Steelhead Drift Fishing

By Bill Luch

Illustrations by Jeff Dayne

Cover photo: Dennis Mobley with winter
run steelhead, photo by Frank W. Amato

FRANK AMATO PUBLICATIONS
Box 82112, Portland, Oregon 97282

ABOUT THE AUTHOR:

Bill Luch is not only an outstanding fisherman, he is also an outstanding sport fisheries conservationest. Bill is a past president of the Association of Northwest Steelheaders and also Trout Unlimited.

I bear witness to the fact that many substantial changes in fisheries management in the Northwest have come about because of Bill Luch and the Northwest Steelheaders. You would be surprised to find out how your fishing has been affected for the better by the man and by the sport fishing conservation organizations he has represented.

Frank W. Amato

DEDICATION

This book is dedicated to the members of the Northwest Steelheaders Council of Trout Unlimited in Oregon and Washington who have worked so hard and contributed so much to the protection of the cold water resources of the Pacific Northwest.

Thanks,

Bill Luch

ISBN-0-936608-00-5
Seventh Printing 1989

Contents

Dick Lawson admires a wild, winter steelhead taken from a small Oregon stream before releasing it back into the water. Notice the downward cast eyes of the steelhead. When they are in this position in a photograph it indicates the fish is alive. After killing a steelhead the eyes will move up — Photo by Frank W. Amato

Introduction

Any "how to" book faces one problem from the beginning: To get the message across without boring the reader beyond tolerance. With fishing, you do have the knowledge backing you up that even though nothing is happening right now, the big one is just around the next bend. With luck, that will be the reader's attitude about this book—on the next page may be the small item that will provide more fish to you on each trip.

Don't misunderstand the "more fish" remark. I'm talking about fish landed, not fish killed—there's a vast difference. Releasing fish becomes a habit with the successful fisherman, one that provides many hours of pleasure in his skill, and yet protects for the future the source of his enjoyment.

The most efficient way to fish for anadromous sport fish (steelhead trout, coho and chinook salmon and cutthroat trout) from the banks of the smaller streams of the Northwest is drift fishing. Steelhead trout provide the main fishing for this kind of fishing, but all of the above will respond well to drifting under proper conditions. Drifting for salmon is largely a neglected sport, however, because of the ease and success of fishing from a boat in the salt chuck or the major rivers where these occur.

To the dedicated practitioner of the art of drift fishing, however, nothing compares to the delight of reading the water, feeling the bottom, then the bite, then the fish, on a small stream off the beaten path—then you're as hooked as the fish.

The wonderful thing about this particular aspect of fishing is that it is a year-round sport: Summer steelhead from late March through November; coho and fall chinook from the first rains of fall stretching through early December on some streams; winter steelhead from November through March; spring chinook (elusive but well worth the effort) from May through the first of July.

Now, friends, that is a solid potential for magnificent fishing. Those who bother to spend the time, money and effort to become successful drift fishermen are rewarded with some of the finest fishing anywhere on earth. Really, it is never the number of fish you catch that is important, but the quality of fish that counts. The amount of skill and knowledge needed to put the fish on the bank goes a long way toward making that quality.

The purpose of this book is to be as straight and simple as possible in explaining the art of drift fishing. The book is written with the fisherman in mind who

7

has no equipment and has never fished this way before. Because of this, many will find thoughts or ideas here they already know of or that they may disagree with. The things I have to say are gleaned from more than 30 years of serious fishing for anadromous fish. But, let me emphasize this: If what you do on the stream is successful for you—don't change because of something I write here! It's what works for you that counts.

Starting with the single-action fly reel and hand coiled line to the belly basket and on through the modern spinning and casting reels, drift fishing has improved in efficiency and ease as equipment has become more technologically perfect. It is with the big break-through—the new reels and light, sensitive glass rods—that this book will be dealing.

There are many myths about drift fishing, both among fishermen and in the marketplace. If, in my opinion, an old saw is a myth or a popular marketplace item fits that category, I intend to say so. In 30 years or so of practice I admit to forming certain opinions and prejudices, and they will surely creep into this text. No apology will be made or is intended for this, as these opinions have, in all honesty, helped me to find and land many a fish.

The beginner at drift fishing makes many mistakes. Most of these will teach him something and become part of the learning of the art. One mistake commonly made by the novice that actually hinders his progress is what I call "shotgunning". Starting out for winter steelhead, the novice is eager and excited—he fishes four different streams on his first four days of fishing. Many fishermen continue this tactic, always wondering why their success ratio is not nearly as good as the next guy's. They are breaking a cardinal rule of good drift fishing—don't shotgun!

Pick a stream, then narrow that down to four or five good drifts, then learn them—I mean *learn* them. Study them at low water to find out what the bottom is like, watch the other fishermen and mark where you see fish hooked. Hit that spot first next trip.

The first rule is "know your water"; break it and you remain a greenhorn; follow it, and you're well on your way to success.

There is an old saw that says: "80% of the fish are caught by 10% of the fishermen." The purpose of this book will be to help you change that ratio.

CHAPTER ONE

Equipment

There is an old saying going back some 2,000 years that holds that "the Gods do not subtract the time a man spends fishing." The amount of success you enjoy will be subtracted, though, in ratio to the lack of time you spend on preparing for fishing.

The purchase of the necessary gear for drift fishing is a very personal thing, and no one can outfit you but yourself. The things to look for can be listed and evauluations made, or suggested, but in the final analysis we all have to choose our own gear to fit us as individuals.

The rules of any marketplace apply and should be followed as closely as the pocketbook will allow. There is no substitute for quality, and, although price is not always an indicator, it is a good guideline. It stands to reason that a rod priced at $15 will have better workmanship than one priced at $5.

This is not to say that a $5 rod won't work for you—it probably will. But how long? How much chance is there of failure at a critical time? Is this cheap rod able to perform as well as the more expensive one? These are questions you must decide before you buy.

Quality tackle purchased carefully and given reasonable maintenance will last a lifetime. I have rods that go back too many years to talk about, and they perform today as well as they did the first time out.

Something else you might consider is that different water and different fish take their own individual gear. I know many one-rod fishermen. I was a one-rodder at one time. Not any more. Each situation calls for something special, within reason, and the pleasure and success increase with their use.

To illustrate, consider fishing steelhead trout in winter on the Clackamas River in Oregon. The same gear used would get you by on the Clackamas tributary, Eagle Creek, but really, now, you don't need that large water rod on Eagle Creek. The Clackamas demands an 8½- to 9-foot rod in order to cover the water. Eagle Creek can be covered easily with 7-7½ feet of rod, with much less trouble packing it through the brush.

Surely cutthroat trout don't demand the gear that fall chinook or coho require. So you will find yourself, as you become more and more addicted, gathering an ever-increasing number of rods, reels and other paraphernalia. One excuse is to have sons who always require more gear. I offer no advice on how to solve this problem with the distaff side other than shouting louder than she can or taking her with you and selling her on how much gear she needs (that you can use).

RODS

Long, short, one-piece, two-piece, heavy, light, fast tip, stiff tip, magnum, classic, long-handled, short-handled, reel seal, tape on reel—enough to drive you nuts and then some. Where to from here?

ROD ACTION

To begin with, let's discuss action and what makes it, why it's important, and go on from there. Generally speaking there are two main classifications for drift rod action: classic (full action) and magnum (concentrated action). See page 11.

Classic action denotes that the rod is so built that the arc or bow of the rod is more or less uniform from tip to butt. This comes with varying degrees of moderation, of course, but as you see on page 11, the arc is generally in the rod and all of the rod is used to provide it.

Magnum action describes those rods built so that 60 to 70 percent of the arc or bow is in the forward half of the rod. From the tip back about half the length, you have a slow taper, then from there to the butt the taper quickens to provide a tough, firm butt section and a fast, flexible tip.

With the classic action all of the rod works for you all of the time—whether fighting a fish or casting. With magnum action the forward section carries most of the work load. Both types have their place, and each fisherman swears his rod action is the best. And, of course, it is, especially if he has fitted his rod action to: 1) the fish he's after, and 2) the water he's fishing.

I use a magnum rod for summer steelhead almost all the time because I want the quick recovery that the magnum provides to handle the speed and acrobatics of these fish. I use a magnum rod on small streams to take advantage of the easy wrist-flick cast with very small weights.

For general fishing or for a fisherman just beginning the best bet is a classic action. Most beginners start fishing on larger streams with easier access, and here the classic shines. It provides good action for long casts. It handles fish easily and takes up the slack when a mistake is made. The light action classic (there are stiff actions, too) provides good feel of the bottom and plenty of backbone to set the hook or pull off of a snag.

One of the most important items to look for when purchasing your rod (regardless of type of action) is the number and placement of the guides. Their importance comes from a good solid rule about rods: The rod fights the fish. You handle the rod, but that rod must fight the fish—if it doesn't then the line does, and you are in trouble. The only way you get by with light lines while drift fishing is by using a rod that will compensate by taking the weight and action of the fish away from the line.

To provide for this kind of support the guides must be placed in such a manner that the line follows the arc of the rod as closely as possible. This will occur when sufficient guides are used and placement is correct. Any rod of seven feet or longer with less than six guides just will not provide this feature. I personally prefer seven guides (counting the tip). A good rule to follow is one guide for each foot of rod.

When you are shopping for your rod, place a reel on the rod and thread the line through the guides. Page 12 shows you what to look for.

STEELHEAD DRIFT ROD ACTIONS

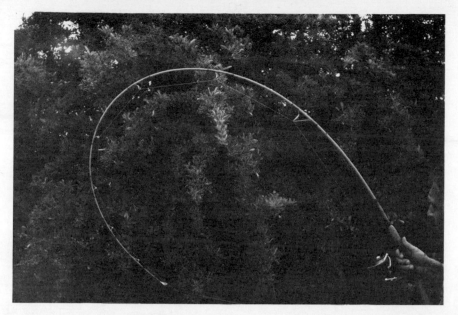

CLASSIC ACTION: Arc extends through most of rod

MAGNUM ACTION: Arc is primarily in the tip

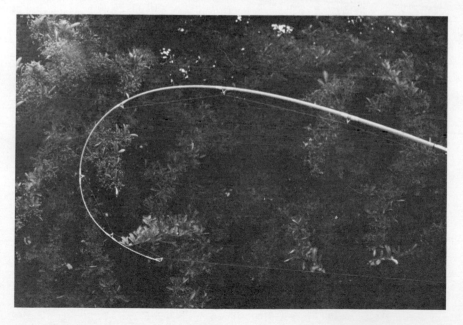

Stay away from the longbow effect as this will not provide the type of action you need for drift fishing.

SPACING OF GUIDES

Another key factor is the distance from the front of the reel to the first guide. When casting, the line leaves the spool of a spinning reel in loops. These loops flatten out as they get farther from the reel, and that first guide must be far enough away, and large enough, to take the loops with a minimum of friction and compression. Incorrect placement or too small a diameter cuts into casting distance. The distance from the face of the reel to the first guide should be more than 24 inches.

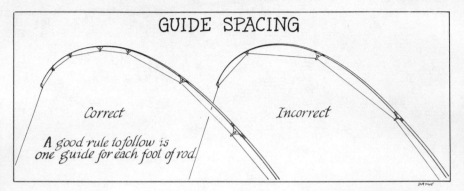

GUIDE SPACING

Correct

Incorrect

A good rule to follow is one guide for each foot of rod.

ROD LENGTH

When you discuss rod lengths you immediately become caught by one question: "What will the rod be used for?" If you are a small stream fisherman, as I am, you surely don't want a nine-foot stick to blunder about through the brush with. So let's talk of maximum and minimum lengths, and then you can choose for your own needs.

A drift rod of under seven feet is not (in most cases) adequate for all-around fishing. In the first place a short rod usually has a short handle, and for drift fishing the long handle is really a necessity. A good cork handle that, when the reel is held for casting, extends up the forearm to near the elbow provides support that is sorely needed. A day of casting and retrieving with a good fight at (we hope) frequent intervals will prove this value in a hurry. So, unless you are looking for the exotic (like some of the little midge rods), seven feet is about as short as you would want. At the outside, nine feet is enough. I have had longer and seen many longer than this, but ended up not using the really long ones; I found they just were not necessary. They didn't provide any additional efficiency, and they were the devil to pack around.

One-piece or two-piece? Really a matter of preference. I prefer one-piece rods because of their better action, but a two-piece rod that is well made will do a good job any time. When you break a rod for a ferrule you naturally take away some of the freedom of action of that rod, especially a classic action rod. But, a rod that is well constructed and has the correct taper will handle this with a minimum of action loss. Choose with care, and you won't go wrong.

ROD CARE

Any piece of equipment needs care. Your rod, given good care, should last you a lifetime. Glass rods manufactured today for drift fishing are mostly of the hollow glass type. As such, they are very prone to damage from car doors, banging against rocks and being pinched. Take care, for many a trip has been ruined by a careless foot or car door. After fishing wipe your rod down with a soft, damp cloth or paper towel to remove the oils from handling and any dried bait residue that always seems to collect. At least once every two years your rod should be wiped with a good thinner, cleaned and the wrapping threads given a coat or two of good rod varnish. Only the threads need this care, but the coat should be carried about a half-inch beyond them.

WRAPPING FRAYED GUIDES

Any sign of fraying on the wrappings should be dealt with immediately. Remove the frayed thread, gently sand and clean away the built-up varnish, then rewrap. This page shows you the proper way to wrap your rod. If you don't feel like doing this yourself, many sporting goods stores will provide this service or give you information on where to go to get this work done. If you do it yourself make your wrappings tight and close together (a tool to aid you can be purchased inexpensively at most sporting goods stores). Apply at least three coats of color preserver and two coats of rod varnish.

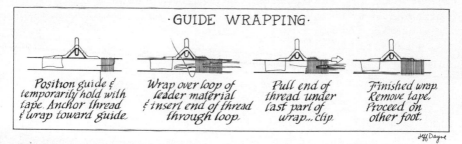

·GUIDE WRAPPING·

Position guide & temporarily hold with tape. Anchor thread & wrap toward guide.

Wrap over loop of leader material & insert end of thread through loop.

Pull end of thread under last part of wrap...clip.

Finished wrap. Remove tape. Proceed on other foot.

GROOVED GUIDES

Keep a close watch on your guides (especially the tip) for grooves caused by line action. These are deadly as they will cut your line at the wrong time. Grooved guides or tips must be replaced immediately. A cadmium steel tip will help alleviate this problem, but they are quite brittle and must be treated with care.

I always carry an extra rod and reel with me on any trip, having been burned too many times. However, it also pays to carry a roll of plastic tape (a good emergency substitute for thread), a small tube of ferrule cement and an extra tip at least one size larger than is on your rod, somewhere in your vest for emergency streamside repairs. You may be lucky and never have to use them, but breakdowns always occur at the peak of the run!

THE "FEEL" OF THE ROD

Since one of the main criteria for drift fishing is "feel," the rod you buy must provide this function for you. Many beginners start out with too stiff a rod and suffer because they lose touch with their sinker and, more often, lose the delicate feeling of the bite. Winter steelhead and chinook salmon, in particular, bite very softly. The action of the rod, especially the forward action, must provide for this delicate feeling. A classic action rod, then, must have a delicate tip action—be sure you look for it. This type of action is an integral part of most magnum action rods. It occurs in the way the taper increases. The tip of your rod must provide to both the eye and the hand a sense of what is happening to your bait or lure during the drift. Too stiff a rod will not meet this criteria.

As has already been stated, the purchase of gear is a very personal thing to any fisherman. Use what I have said as a guide for comparison and shop carefully.

SPINNING REELS

By far the greatest number of drift fishermen use the spinning reel. The introduction of this type of reel was probably the greatest breakthrough of all the gear inventions for easy drift fishing.

Of all the gear you will purchase for drift fishing, the reel is the most important. When failures occur with gear it is usually the reel that causes the most consternation and dismay. Several rivers of the Northwest carry on their bottom reels that I have deposited there in moments of utter disgust. So be careful when you buy. One further delineation: The discussion will be on "open faced" spinning reels only. The "closed faced" reel hasn't been made—to my knowledge—that will consistently handle large anadromous fish. If you insist on using one—Good Luck!

THE BRAKE OR "DRAG"

Any spinning reel has one major disadvantage—the line, coming off the spool, must make a ninety-degree turn in order to run the guides. This little development causes extra drag and friction on the line. The direct result here is the necessity for a good brake. Really, the key to any spinning reel is its brake. Ads for spinning reels stress line capacity, ratio of retrieve, collapsibility of handle, etc. Now, what is really important to you, the buyer and fisherman? I list three items as being of major importance, then others carrying lesser values: 1) the brake, 2) the distance from the foot to the body of the reel (in particular the bail), and 3) the type and quality of the gearing. A fourth but lesser value is weight—we'll discuss this later.

First and foremost, the brake: Braking action on most spinning reels is provided by a disk, or series of disks, working against one another to provide friction. Some kind of a screw-down device is used to increase or lessen this friction. Since by its design a spinning reel is severely limited in space, the only way a reel can have its braking area increased (the larger the area, the more efficient the brake) is to increase the number of interacting disks. A point of diminishing returns is quickly reached, however, and you find very few reels with more than six disks. Four is a good number provided they are properly aligned and of suitable material. Like materials don't work well together—remember the old saw about metal to metal contact. So, for really good results, you look for fiber to metal to fiber or a like combination. In my opinion metal to leather forms the best brake disc combination. A point to consider with a reel you are happy with is that leather disks are easily made at home.

Another point about brakes: Sand and dirt are almost impossible to keep out of your reels. Any material used in a brake that is easily scored or gouged and is hard enough that that scoring is not at least partially re-absorbed may cause trouble. Any brake that doesn't run smoothly and surely is an invitation to lost fish. Any brake that runs—that is, doesn't give a consistent action—will also be a problem. Unfortunately, there is no sure test other than on the river under fishing conditions. But put the reel on a rod, run the line through the guides and have a salesman or buddy play fish. Watch that reel under various tensions for slippage, grabbing or catching, etc., before you buy.

SIZE OF THE REEL

Now about that distance from the foot to the body. Everyone has a difference in size of their hands. When you grasp your rod for the cast and retrieve the size and thickness of your hand and fingers must be taken into account. What misery to make a trip and then discover that with every turn of the handle the bail smacks you smartly on the knuckle of your forefinger. You end up with a bloody knuckle or a vastly uncomfortable grip (inefficient, too) from then on when you use that reel. Make sure the leg of the reel is long enough for you before you buy.

THE REEL GEARS

Gears: The best bet here is to follow some general rules that apply to all gearing: 1. Metal beats fiber hands down! 2. Cut gears are much better than

Steelhead caught with a spinning reel. — Photo by Les Johnson

stamped, also more expensive! 3. Ball bearings are nice but not necessary. 4. The play between the gears is a good indication of quality—sloppy gears will wear much faster. 5. Gears need grease—don't be chintzy. Take off a side plate and fill the gear box with a good grade of silicone grease. Clean this out with solvent at least once a year and refill with grease.

When I buy a new reel I take it to a friend who is a machinist and have him run lapping compound on the gears. He then takes down any high or rough spots. This little extra trouble provides a huge improvement in smoothness of action. This is what you're really after in your reel—smooth, sure, substantial action. With care and maintenance your reel will outlast your years of hopping from rock to rock.

WEIGHT OF REEL

The weight of a reel is not of major importance, but consider this: It doesn't make sense to put a midge type reel on a nine-foot rod. Nor does the seven-foot magnum need a 300-yard capacity reel. You will know at the end of a day's fishing whether the reel you have bought is too clubby. Your arm will tell you in no uncertain terms.

LEVEL WIND REELS

A mini-revolution has been taking place in steelhead fishing technique during the last ten years or so. Ten years ago you seldom saw a level wind casting reel on the river. The spinning reel was used by 90% of the fishermen. Today on the rivers the use of casting reels has increased to nearly half the fishermen.

Casting reels provide two elements not well provided by a spinning reel: They give you much surer control over both your gear and the fish, and they are not subject to the swift and unexpected breakdowns that many spinning reels provide with no notice.

The modern level wind bait casting reel has evolved, over the years, into an instrument providing fine, watch-like, internal mechanics as well as a sure-fire, almost foolproof brake system. Combine these features with ease of disassembly, good line capacity and quick spool change, and you have a very precise, convenient fishing reel.

The older models of bait casting reels had, in most cases, no face spool, no brake and no level wind. The modern reels include all of these plus a centrifugal casting brake to control overspin during the cast as well as spool brake adjustments to limit the need of extra thumb pressure.

Most casting reels have a "star drag" type of brake system consisting of a series of disks (washers) tightened against the spool plate by a wheel at the reel handle. The braking system on almost all makes of these reels are superb and cause very little trouble.

One area where the casting reel is better than the spinning reel is in the lack of friction. The line comes off the spool of a spinning reel making a right-angle turn at the bail. The line from a casting reel moves straight down the rod from the spool. Because of this you can wind against a fish even when not retrieving line without fear of line twist (and a later break). This feature alone makes it worth taking the trouble to learn to operate a casting reel.

By the way, there will be some trouble! About the only sure way to convert

Steelhead caught with a casting reel. — Photo by Les Johnson

to a casting reel is to leave the spinning gear at home and fight the backlash battle for a season. With no temptation to reach for the spinning outfit, you grit your teeth and continue. Remember that with the advent of centrifigal casting brakes and automatic thumbing brakes the reel manufacturers have made the old casting reel much easier for the beginner to master.

The only area where a casting reel falls short is on a brushy stream where full back cast movement is restricted or when casting ultra-light weights—under these conditions the spinning reel shines.

It would be a shame to talk about reels and casting without covering an old, old method that is enjoying a mini-revival in some areas and deserves to be more widely used. I am referring to the fine old art of stripping.

Stripping gear consists of an eight to nine-foot fly rod, a single-action fly reel with fifty yards or so main line and fifty to a hundred yards of dacron backing. The main line that works best is the flat mono called Cobra marketed by Cortland Line Co. of Cortland, New York. Cobra is a flat monofilament that resists tight looping and will lay out in loose, non-tangling coils when stripped from the reel. The twenty-pound test Cobra seems to work the best of all the line weights, so your backing should be twenty-pound, or better still 25-pound dacron.

The terminal tackle is the same as any other drift gear; the difference lies in casting and retrieving only.

The technique requires you to strip from the reel the line necessary to make your cast, making certain that the line coils in such a way as to be free to run through the guides during the cast. On a small stream this is relatively simple because of short casting distance. On bigger water you may have to add the old standby—a belly basket. Simply a box or basket fastened around the waist with a belt, the belly basket provides a resting place for the coils of line stripped from the reel and helps prevent tangles.

Casting is done side arm with the line feeding through the off-rod hand and out through the guides. The reel is used only to fight a fish or wind in after fishing a spot out. All other retrieving while fishing is done by stripping in the line—recoiling it for another cast. Strip fishing is slower than a spin or casting reel operation, but many of us tend to fish too fast; the slower pace is much to the good. You will be surprised at the number of strikes that come as you strip line in at the end of a drift, moving your gear back up through the drift in an erratic and jerky manner. You will also find that you have very sure and sensitive control of your gear as it passes through the drift constantly picking up or letting out line as you maneuver your sinker. By the way, I've seen many types of belly baskets used, but the best I ever had was a wicker creel with the top removed—it was light, was big enough and easy to buckle around the waist. Try it—you'll have a ball.

HOW MUCH LINE?

In all of the years I have fished I have never had a steelhead or salmon take out 150 yards of line on me. One hundred-fifty yards is a very great distance on any stream. Any fish that takes that kind of line length away from you is a goner—he's around the bend and on his way! The point is that line capacity over say, 200 yards of 8- or 10-pound test is mostly a waste of good line. It will never get used. I don't even own a reel with a capacity of more than about 180 yards of 8-pound test.

Here is one way to fill your reel so that you can change your line from time to time with a minimum of bother: wind onto your reel 100 yards of whatever line strength you plan to fish with, then tie on backing line with the test increased by half (with 6-pound use 10, with 8-pound use 12, and so on). Fill the reel to within one-eighth inch of the lip of the spool (approximately). Now, either wind this onto another spool of the same size for that reel or stretch it out (good work for your wife here—kind of makes her part of the next trip—without having to actually take her along), reverse and rewind onto your spool. This provides you with backing that will last for years and easy replacement of the line you have in constant use, using only 100 yards at a time.

Another precaution is to buy extra spools for each of your reels. Fill them with varying weights of lines and make sure you always have a spare with you. An extra spool is an inexpensive way to double the use of your reel for heavier fish or bigger water. Two or three extra spools will expand for you not only the use of your reel but, also, if you tape your reel on rather than use a rod with a reel seat will make it much easier to double the rod.

ROD AND REEL BALANCE

Try to purchase your reel with a balance between reel and rod in mind. In fact, it pays to take the rod along when shopping for your reel to achieve this. Although these things may sound trivial to the beginner—over the years you will find, as I have, that these seemingly small things add a great deal to fishing skill and thus to your enjoyment of the sport.

I'm going to repeat the bit about grease because it is so important. Grease the reel heavily—both in the gear housing and in the brake. Anywhere there appears to be any friction in the works of your reel, use grease. Get a good brand of silicone grease that will maintain its working ability in cold weather. One brand I have found to be excellent is put out by Garcia. I usually go through at least one tube per reel at each cleaning.

DROPPING THE REEL

If you should accidentally drop your reel in the sand, clean it then and there. Don't wait 'til too late when irreparable damage may have occurred. Rinse it in fresh water and dry it off, then open it up (or remove the spool, depending on the amount of sand picked up) and clean it out as thoroughly as possible before re-use. All the care in the world used while buying will go for nothing if you are careless during actual use.

Pioneer steelhead fisherman on the Sandy River, Oregon.
— Oregon Historical Society photo

One further item: Check your gear prior to purchase as carefully as possible. Don't hesitate to look hard and thoroughly at what you are buying. Your own eyes and hands will tell you best, that salesman may never have fished for steelhead trout before. If he doesn't want to take a reel down for your inspection—*go somewhere else!* If you buy carefully and look for quality you will most likely be spending somewhere between $30 and $50 on rod and reel. You are entitled to know exactly what you're getting for your money.

HOOKS, LINES AND SINKERS

Talk about a bewildering array of tackle! Well, here it is. There are so many brands, types, styles, weights—and on and on—that anyone can get confused. There are some general rules to follow, yes, but mostly it will end up with what works for you.

For instance: No one can tell you how much sinker to use—it changes all the time due to water conditions, bait or lure used, line weight, etc. Almost any type of light, easily fastened-on lead can be used. I personally prefer the hollow type pencil leads that can be pinched on a short dropper line. Some use a three-way swivel and surgical tubing, others a pencil lead tied on the dropper line; others split shot or other clamp-on types. They all will work equally well. It really boils down to what you consider fast and convenient.

HOW MUCH LEAD TO USE

The amount used, however, is a different thing. Here the only sure decision must be made at the drift. At first it is a matter of judgment, but one cast should tell you whether or not you are too heavy or light. Since your gear must get to the bottom, yet continue to move, the weight is extremely important. If I am on strange water I always try to start a little heavy. It is much easier to pinch off a bit of lead than to add more. What you are aiming for is a constant movement of your gear through the drift without losing contact with the bottom for more than a couple of feet at a time. Too much lead and you're hung up all the time—too little and you have no drift; it's that simple. Still, a great number of fishermen never figure this out—they don't hook many fish, either.

HOOKS

The range of hooks available to the drift fisherman is so varied that it could be incomprehensible to the beginner. The following diagram illustrates how hooks are sized and some descriptive terms.

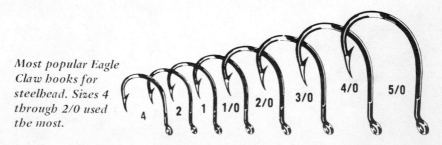

Most popular Eagle Claw hooks for steelhead. Sizes 4 through 2/0 used the most.

No. 182 Extra strong short shank up eye

Generally the size I prefer for both winter and summer steelhead is a 2/0. For salmon in the fall I go to a 3/0 and during the low, clear water of late summer steelhead fishing I often drop down to a 4 for use with single eggs or nightcrawlers. In the original edition of this book I talked about hooks in the 1 and 2 size range. Well, frankly, friends, I lost too many fish from hooks coming unpinned and have found the larger hooks much more effective.

Buy hooks that do not have a bait holding slice like this one does.

Try to buy hooks without a bait holding slice if you can because they interfere with the tying of an egg loop. At any rate use pliers to pinch them down before tying or they may cut your line. Also, an up-eyed hook will serve you better if you tie your own rigs because it keeps the point of the hook clear of the bait.

A good test for hook quality is to flick the point with your thumbnail as hard as you can—if it bends, don't buy! Keep those hooks *sharp!* This calls for constant checking. Two or three scrapes against a rock will blunt the best hooks around. Carry a small file or stone and use it frequently.

If you bend your hook out of shape on a snag, don't bend it back and re-use it. When bought by the box of 100 they will probably cost you between 2 and 3 cents each. Why lose a fish for that amount of money? Cut a damaged hook off and replace it.

LINE

Monofilament line is judged two ways: Diameter and tested strength. Naturally, the smaller the diameter the less the tested strength of the line. The main consideration of diameter concerns the amount of drag in the water and the suppleness of the line. Preferably, line for a spinning reel should be soft and very supple, with potential to stretch before breaking. For bait casting reels the line should be stiffer. The extra stiffness helps cut down on backlashes. There are lines on the market with some or most of the stretch removed. I consider the ability of my line to stretch very important. I want that extra bit working for me.

The larger diameter lines (and heavier pound test) have one drawback to drift fishing: They have more drag and thus lead to more bellying of line. A belly in your line means less fish any time.

How about weight factors? Frankly, I have seldom found it necessary to go below six-pound test for winter or summer steelhead trout. Conversely, twelve-pound test is plenty heavy for these fish under almost any conditions. I once read a story in one of the national "sport" magazines about the use of thirty-pound test for winter steelhead on small, northern California streams. The excuse was the heavy brush. Why not use a winch and good half-inch cable? There would be just as much sport and all the excitement of perhaps breaking a sheer pin.

Cutthroat trout fished with spinning gear do not require line this heavy. Drop down to four-pound or less. Salmon, however, are a different breed of cat. Now you must go high enough to hold these large fish but stay light enough to cast easily. I have found that twelve to fifteen-pound test in the spring works well, and fifteen to twenty-pound test will handle almost any fall fish given the right kind of rod and reel. Again, the rod fights the fish, not the line. Try running six-pound test line on a good supple rod and tying the end onto a heavy (twenty pounds or so) weight. Now, try to break the line by other means than a straight pull or a snap. If you have trouble, think of the trouble a fish will have.

Here are some hints about hooks, lines and sinkers: Try buying your lead in bulk rolls (hollow pencil lead comes this way in most stores). Buy your line in bulk amount, too, rather than 100 yards at a time. English and American steel hooks are very good, but in my opinion the best is still the old reliable Mustad. Try the Mustad No. 92550 size 2/0 for steelhead and No. 92553 size 3/0 for salmon.

Learn to tie your own gear; it's a good way to pass a rainy evening and will cut down on the amount of your overall cost of fishing. Page 27 shows you some of the knots and ties to use when making up your own sets.

In summary: Buy good quality and shop hard for what you buy. Then give your equipment good maintenance. Keep your rod and reel clean and the reel well lubricated. Balance your equipment as well as you can to fit your needs and use extra spools for your reel to double the uses of your gear. Often it is the "little" things given attention that add so much to success and pleasure.

CHAPTER TWO

Rigging—Bait or Lure

Regardless of what kind of sport you enter, you immediately begin some form of competition. In that competition the type, quality, quantity and understanding of your equipment will often have a direct influence on your success. Don't think for one minute that you don't compete when you fish. Competition occurs between fishermen, between fishermen and nature and, above all, between fishermen and the fish. What better competition is there in fishing than that between a fifteen-pound fish and you with a six-pound test line?

No matter what combination of gear you use, though, the odds are against you. Sooner or later you'll find the right combination of luck and circumstance and hook your quarry. It follows that you must attempt to remove as much of this "chance" factor as you possibly can. You can have the finest rod, reel, line, etc., available and still be relying too heavily on chance. The selection of proper bait, correct lure and a workable tie-up will help you go beyond luck and circumstance to a point of maximum return for your investment, both in time and money.

Among many fishermen the combination of terminal tackle used is called the "rig". "How were you rigged?" or "What kind of rig were you using?" are questions you often hear. So when I discuss rig or rigging you must understand that I am talking about that portion of your tackle from swivel to hook. How you make this rigging work for you to its best advantage, what works better or best under what conditions, and how this is all put together will now be discussed.

RIGGING

The basis for all of this discussion is that section of your gear from swivel down, and how it is put together. But first some background:

The very purpose of drift fishing is to cover the water holding the fish as completely as possible. To do this you must follow some hard rules. First, your gear must move through the drift while staying in close contact with the bottom. Second, you must cover the water where the fish will most likely be. We'll discuss these facts more fully in a later chapter.

Most rigs used in drift fishing are basically the same. That is, they begin with a swivel, have a length of leader and end with a hook for use with bait or some type of lure. Included is a dropper line or some other type of device that a sinker can be attached to. A floating type of lure can be added or the hook removed and a spoon or spinner attached, but the basics remain the same.

Many fishermen advocate a dropping of test strength between the line and the leader. Fine, if you wish, but not necessary. The main reason for this is to provide for breakage at the leader instead of up the main line in case of a snag. This makes sense except that you have three knots between the hook and main line—at the hook and at each end of the swivel. Any knot or bend (knotless tie) in monofilament line will reduce the strength of that line by at least five to fifteen percent. This being the case, then the breaking point is built into any rig—three of them, in fact. Given a main line without flaws, the rig will break at one of the ties—most likely those at the swivel. So, to me, it doesn't make much sense to carry around special leader material when the line you are using will do just as well. It does make sense, however, to carry already-prepared rigs with you so that you are not cannibalizing your main line to tie up new gear.

On page 25 you will find a typical drift rig tied up for bait fishing. The same form may be used for any set-up and is used to show the basic tie-up. I use this rig both for its simplicity and versatility. It's easy to tie and quick and very adaptable. The tail line at the swivel is for the sinker. It is not tied separately, but is part of the knot to the leader, and I use it with hollow pencil lead that I simply pinch on. This type of lead slides off easily under pressure and will save many a rig from snag loss. When I tie this outfit onto my main line, I leave a tail there also to provide a spot to hang an extra length of lead if I find a little more is needed.

EGG HOOKS

The picture on page 27 shows a simple egg hook tie-up. Probably the most basic of all rigs, it is also the most widely used among drift fishermen. The hook is tied in such a way as to provide for a loop between the eye of the hook and the snell that will hold the eggs securely against the shank. If the eggs are properly cured, they will remain in place for several drifts.

Of major importance with an egg (or artificial egg-type lure) rig is the length of leader. Many beginners start out with too long a leader. I have become convinced, over the years, that a long distance between the sinker and the hook is not only unnecessary but detrimental. To understand what I mean you must visualize the action of your gear during the drift. The sinker (close to the swivel at the top of the tie-up) will travel behind the bait as it proceeds through the drift, held back by both weight and contact with the bottom. Downstream from it you find the bait. If you are using a 30-inch leader, let's say, you should analyze what happens when the bait is picked up by a fish. Winter steelhead and chinook, in particular, bite softly. Most of the time these fish will pick up the bait in passing and simply mouth it for a short time. Since there is no real direct pull on the line, an inexperienced fisherman seldom picks out the very subtle change that occurs in the action of the drift. Most fishermen do not recognize this gentle "feel" until their sinker has traveled far enough past the fish to exhaust the length of the leader. The gear then stops, the fisherman picks up on his line and—lo and behold—a fish.

What happens, then, with that 30-inch leader? If the bait is directly downstream from the sinker when it is picked up, that sinker must travel 60 inches or five feet before the fish is discovered! That is way too far. It is said that the

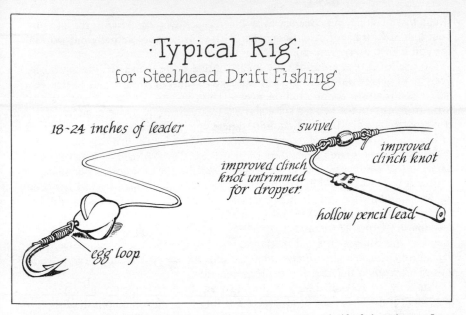

·Typical Rig·
for Steelhead Drift Fishing

18-24 inches of leader

swivel

improved clinch knot

improved clinch knot untrimmed for dropper.

hollow pencil lead

egg loop

majority of steelhead fishermen never feel as many as one-half of their bites. I know this was the case with me, and it took me long hours of hard fishing before I became adept at reading the "feel" of a bite.

Years ago, on a small, brushy stream in California, my fishing partner and I experimented with this phenomenon. It was possible to crawl out onto the willows that grew over the water on this stream and watch the steelhead as they passed under them seeking safety. We used to take white thread and tie on a gob of eggs. This we would attach to a short stick. Then, with the aid of a face mask we would manipulate the eggs hanging on the thread so that we could literally bump them on the fishes' noses. Most of these fish would pick up the eggs. One out of every six or eight would swallow them. By far the greatest number simply lipped or mouthed the eggs for four or five seconds and spit them out.

It went kind of like this—chomp, chomp, chomp, ptewiee—and away went the eggs. Now we didn't have a hook hanging with those eggs and often the fishes' attempt to expell them under actual conditions causes the hook to do its work. But, given the short time these fish held the eggs and the fact that during this time they didn't move, it is easier to see the importance of leader length. My advice is never go longer than 24 inches. Personally, I have a set length I use. I hold my tied hook between thumb and forefinger and tie on my swivel at the point on the leader even with my elbow. For me that is 18½ inches, and I use it constantly.

Reducing the amount of sinker travel, after a fish mouths the bait, from five feet to less than three feet can make quite a difference in your success.

Page 27 shows you some of the ties to use when preparing your gear. A simple, improved clinch knot is the easiest and quickest to use at the swivel or when tying on a lure. It only cuts line strength about 15 percent and, properly tied, will not come apart. It is fast. Speed is not something you consistently think about when fishing, but consider this: No fish are ever caught with the end of your line in your hand. Any time spent with your gear not actually out working for you is time away from your fishing.

No one loves to stand and contemplate nature more than I. But being thigh-deep in 40-degree water and the rest exposed to rain, snow or a cool 15-degree breeze is not a time conducive to contemplation. When you have a bright silver form fresh out on the bank, a smoke and a toddy from the thermos in hand—contemplate away! If the action didn't warm you, go home—it's too damn cold to fish.

What I am promoting is a system of priorities. To be forced by lack of preparation to tie up a new bait rig from scratch at the drift is idiotic. The same with snags. To spend ten dollars' worth of fishing time trying to save a fifty-cent rig (and spooking the drift in the process) is worse than idiotic. Most steelhead (and salmon and cutthroat) rigging comes ready made for you, in all sizes, styles and line strengths. This book shows a very representative group. Many fishermen buy the components and tie their own. I prefer this way because over the years I have honed and perfected what I use to the point that only I can provide a finished product that satisfies my requirements.

Primarily, I have aimed for simplicity, speed—both in make-up and when replacement is needed at the drift—and the ability to attract and hold the fish. Don't be misled, however. The gear tied for you by reputable manufacturers will do the job very satisfactorily.

BAIT

Natural bait gets the widest use in drift fishing among the most experienced fishermen. Of all the types available, eggs (or roe) taken from steelhead, coho or chinook salmon receive by far the widest acceptance.

PREPARING FRESH EGGS

Fresh eggs to be used for drift fishing must be properly prepared both for use and for storage. Every fisherman I know has his own "favorite" recipe for preparing them. Here is mine:

The ingredients needed are: 1) the eggs to prepare, 2) borax (not Boraxo but pure borax), 3) brown sugar, and 4) containers.

Pour some of the borax onto some spread-out newspapers and roll the eggs in this until well coated. Add a small amount of borax to the skeins and leave (covered lightly by a piece of newspaper) in a cool place to drain. I prefer my basement for this but many use a refrigerator. Here timing is important. What you are doing is removing excess moisture from the eggs. If they are left too long they become hard and of little use. With roe from steelhead the time will be less than for coho, and both are less than with chinook. Also, the colder you keep them, the slower they will drain. The size of the eggs (maturity) will affect the time needed. Usually about twelve hours will suffice for steelhead; somewhat more time is necessary for each of the species of salmon. Now you must prepare the baits. Using scissors, snip the eggs into baits.

I like a bait about the size of the end of my thumb back to the beginning of the nail. When cutting your baits be careful to include some of the toughened

Knots
for Steelhead drift fishing

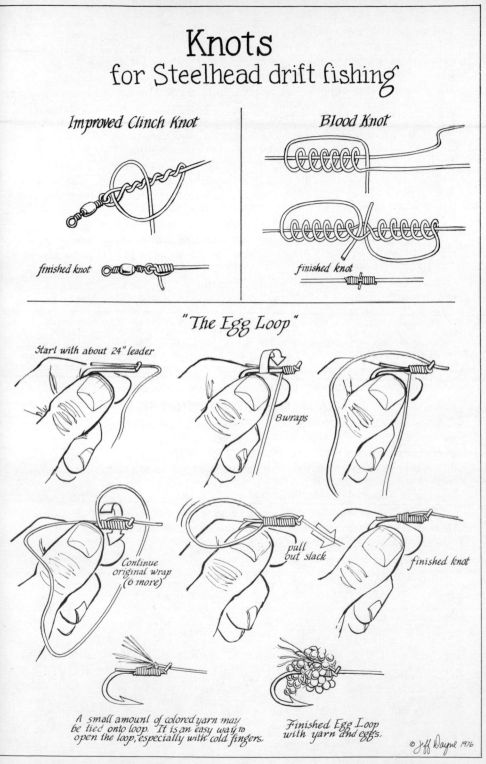

Improved Clinch Knot

finished knot

Blood Knot

finished knot

"The Egg Loop"

Start with about 24" leader

8 wraps

Continue original wrap (6 more)

pull out slack

finished knot

A small amount of colored yarn may be tied onto loop. It is an easy way to open the loop, especially with cold fingers.

Finished Egg Loop with yarn and eggs.

© Jeff Dayne 1976

skin surrounding the skein on each bait. This is needed to help hold them together during use. Also, when removing the eggs from a fish, be very careful to get all of this protective covering with them that you can. Roll these cut-up pieces into the borax gently so that they are thoroughly coated. Now place about one-half inch of borax, mixed eight parts to one with the brown sugar, over the bottom of your container and drop in a layer of baits, more sugared borax, more baits, until the top layer of baits, which should be covered about one inch deep in sugared borax. These eggs may be stored under refrigeration for many weeks or they may be frozen for up to nine months. Eggs frozen in January will keep their consistency through the fall salmon fishing. I have kept them longer, but they are not prime past the eighth or ninth month. The brown sugar is not a necessary ingredient, but acts as a color preserver and heightener. I prefer the brilliance it adds to the redness of the eggs.

When I am fishing water with "color" in it, I prefer to start with eggs. If the "color" is high, I often add a floating type lure such as a "Corky". I tie my rigs especially for this with a "Corky" added to the leader before I put on the swivel. This rig is tied with an egg hook and provides two options—the Corky by itself in clearer waters or eggs on with it to add color to my bait. The Corky dropped free onto the leader will be held right down against the eye of the hook by the action of the current during the drift.

The clearer the water, the smaller the bait used. Many times in low, clear water, two single eggs slipped over the hook will suffice. The key to good eggs is the right combination of toughness and residual juice or "milk". Too juicy a bait will not hold together, while one that is too tough or dry will not "milk out" during a drift. This "milking out" is a factor in attracting the fish.

CRAWFISH TAILS OR SHRIMP

Crawfish tails and shrimp provide successful baits for the steelhead angler, but are neglected by many. Summer steelhead and cutthroat trout are especially fond of these baits. I have never tried them for coho or chinook, but suspect they would work well here, too. For winter fish I like to add a little yarn to my gear for color when using tails. Try pinching off a couple of inches of yarn, doubling it, and tying it to your leader. Slide this down to the eye of the hook and let the ends dangle around the bait. (This works well with eggs and worms, also.) The tails may be threaded directly onto the hook or hung in the egg loop with the hook buried in one end.

WORMS

Once while fishing one of the streams in southwest Washington, a nightcrawler gave my partner and me a good laugh. The trip had been unsuccessful through about 10 a.m. I had tapped one fish, and held him for less than a minute. Other than the vicarious excitement of watching some jerk go blasting out through the very area in which I had hooked the fish, nothing much had happened. My partner of the day was an excellent fisherman, with one serious weakness (now corrected): He used nothing but hardware. As far as he was concerned, if a spinner or wobbler didn't take fish, there weren't any fish around. As we walked up the road covering ground between drifts, I found a nightcrawler stretched out in an attempt to find soft ground among all that macadam. Picking

*Dick Williamson with bright, fresh-run winter
steelhead from a small Oregon coastal stream.*

it up and dropping it into my bait box, I made several remarks to the point that here was my next fish. In the 100 yards or so we had to walk, I listened to strangled laughter and poorly choked guffaws every step of the way. The "meat" is that at the next drift, first cast, worm on and working—"fish on." Now I could tell you that I was a gentleman and didn't say a word, but why lie? I crowed, laughed (cried, too—I lost the fish), hollered, glanced sideways, and generally made a fool of myself for the rest of the day.

Worms work! I know, everyone says, "Great for trout—okay for summer steelhead, but. . .!" Don't pass up nightcrawlers for winter fishing. It's been my experience that the size of a stream plays a large part in the effectiveness of worms as bait in the winter. I have seldom had much luck on large rivers with nightcrawlers. In many instances, on small streams, however, they are deadly.

A good portion of the success with worms comes from how they are presented. Most fishermen, remembering the catfish trips of their youth, will string a worm onto the hook so that the hook is nearly covered. You have this huge gob of worm bunched up and bulging to lay before the fish.

The next time you use nightcrawlers for steelhead (or cutthroat), try hanging the worm on the hook so that at least 80 percent of the worm hangs free. I realize that this will look ridiculous. It works! There is something about that length of worm dangling there that seems to add a great deal of appeal for a steelhead. The trouble you run into is during the cast. With this length of worm hanging and the rest just barely on the hook, any snap in your cast will send the worm on its way—by itself—another reason why larger rivers don't provide prime worm area. So, the cast must be gentle and smooth, with a minimum of whip or snap.

At first glance this rig looks like a built-in invitation for the fish to get three-quarters of a worm free. Such is *not* the case. The fish will take the whole thing or none. One more fact: I have had more genuine "bites" from winter fish on worms than any other bait. Usually I give them three or four taps before setting, but quite often it is a case of swallowed worm and away we go!

GRASSHOPPERS

Most of the anadromous fish streams east of the Cascades in Oregon and Washington are blessed with an abundance of natural bait in the summertime—grasshoppers. One or two of these insects on a hook bumped through a drift can produce some wild times. There isn't much to say about them except: The next time you take a summer fish expedition east of the mountains, carry along a fly swatter. This beats all for capturing these beasts, and it also keeps you off your hands and knees in the brush of rattlesnake country.

LURES

I suppose every fisherman has heard the line about the lure made to catch fishermen, not fish. True enough, I guess, except that steelhead trout and coho salmon, in particular, will take almost anything if it comes to them right, is shiny, wiggles, or smells right.

Lures are broken down by action more than by size or shape, etc. You have those that don't do much of anything but hang there and those that wobble, wiggle or spin. Then, too, you have those that float and those that sink. Regardless of their classification, the same rule always applies: *on the bottom*. These lures must be fished with the same purpose in mind as you had with bait: Cover the water thoroughly and keep your moving contact with the bottom.

FLOATING LURES

I remember when these egg-resembling floating lures first hit the market here in Oregon. I made a trip to California with a dozen or so in my vest. They were unknown in California, and the guys I went fishing with thought I was nuts. That day I hooked six fish in water already bombed with eggs, wobblers, etc. I was promptly offered as high as five bucks each for my remaining tie-ups. Whether I sold or not is my secret. There are many of these types of lures, under a zillion trade names, on the market. I prefer the "Corky" type. I like the diversity of color available and am especially fond of the pearl pink. The general

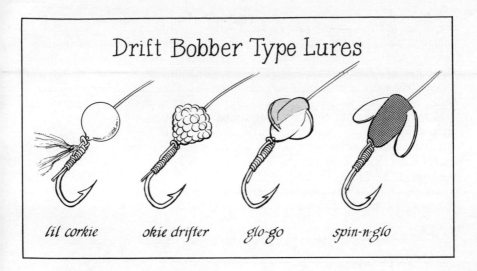

Drift Bobber Type Lures

lil corkie *okie drifter* *glo-go* *spin-n-glo*

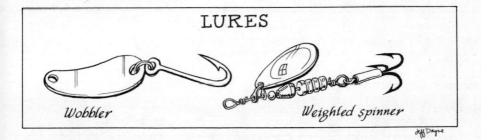

LURES

Wobbler *Weighted spinner*

rule on color is the darker the water color the brighter the lure color—remember, I said, "general rule".

These lures are fished as if they were bait; indeed, they work very well with bait. As I have stated before, two hooks are not necessary, and the action of the current will hold the lure down where it belongs. One factor especially appreciated by the beginner is the little extra flotation provided at the hook. Although these lures don't provide much, they do give just enough lift to keep the hook away from bottom snagging.

There are also floating type lures that have some action to them. Two that come to mind are the Glo-Go and the many flatfish type lures. A small Glo-Go dropped onto a regular egg rig makes a very productive tie. This, too, may be used with eggs or worms or any other bait—or by itself. The current will keep

31

the wings turning so that you can have quite a combination working for you: Movement, color, bait—all at once.

The Glo-Go is also very effective for plunking (still-fishing) larger rivers. The wings provide for a spinning motion that attracts steelhead.

The wigglers—that is, the lures that dive and imitate the actions of a minnow (more or less) can be deadly. They must have weight with them to carry them down during a drift, and they are fished somewhat differently than bait. By that I mean that more tension must be kept on them during the first half of any drift. After your gear begins to move from the point of the cast, and when you are sure you have your bottom-to-bottom pattern, you must keep a slight re-trieve tension on your gear to accent the working of the lure. After about half the drift you usually begin to lose the bottom due to increased pressure from the current. At this time the tension should be let off as the current will take over for you. Any extra pressure here will make you lose bottom and cut your drift. This type of lure is very good for working the tail out of a drift. I'll discuss this in more detail in a later chapter.

Various types of wobblers and weighted spinners, all of which will take steelhead if fished properly. — Photo by Eric Carlisle

SINKING LURES

Several years ago I read of a test conducted by one of the northern states' (Michigan or Minnesota) conservation departments on the hooking qualities of single vs. treble hooks. The results were startling. In almost every series of tests the single hook penetrated farther, deeper and held more solidly than did the treble. Consider this, now: Treble hooks fished on the bottom are snag grabbers without peer. For years I have always removed the treble hook from a lure and replaced it with a siwash-type (straight-shanked) single hook before I used the lure. Sometimes a split-ring is needed to provide for the freedom of the hook, but these are inexpensive and well worth the trouble. Snags will be cut down by at least 50 percent by using a single hook. Most siwash hooks come with an open eye and simply have to be pinched into place with pliers. If my experience is of any value, I can guarantee that you will not lose fish because of this single hook. You will also lose less gear.

Many fishermen, upon using a weighted lure (spinner or wobbler) are convinced that these lures must be pulled through the water in order to work correctly. *Not true!* Drift them through—the current action and a light tension from you will give the lure its chance to work. Spinners do not need to be frantically spinning in order to do their job. They do have to be on the bottom. The flop, flop of the spinner or wobbler as it travels through a drift will provide all the lure action you need to attract the fish. Again the caution about winter fish! They will most often simply stop your lure in its travel without the hard strike of a coho or summer steelhead.

The fisherman who casts and retrieves his spinner or wobbler is a good man to follow on the drift. Unless the water is very clear or the drift is small, the fish under this guy will not be disturbed, and the drift fisherman will take fish right behind him. "Mr. Cast and Retrieve" is a true conservationist, perhaps not from desire but certainly from style. When I discuss water, habitat, casting, etc., in a later chapter, you may get more of an idea about this fact, but it comes down to what the fish needs and how he uses the water to meet these needs. He hugs the bottom, and he utilizes certain kinds of water action in his migration. If you don't go where he is—you lose.

Most of the weighted lures will need extra weight to make them function effectively (depending upon the water). They should never be tied onto the main line. Always use a swivel. I use two, one at the top of my rig, and one at the lure itself. A lure used without a swivel will twist monofilament line into an awful mess.

Understand that my use of the absolute in referring to terminal tackle is a reflection on personal practice. No one can select your favorite rig for you. Favorites come from what produces for you. How you prepare for your trips and what you carry will be constantly refined as you get more and more involved with drift fishing. About once every two or three months I find myself having to go through my vest and rearrange, adding little, discarding quite a lot. This usually occurs when I notice my vest becoming similar to a suitcase packed for a three-week trip.

There is really no excuse for not having enough gear with you on a trip, however, and I am a great one for taking plenty along. When a trip is made to a new stream, I always include extra terminal tackle along with the spare rod and reel. I have run out of rigs a couple of times when the fishing was hot and been forced to tie gear at streamside. What a nerve-wracking thing to hit a drift full of fresh-run fish and lose your last prepared rig. Then, all thumbs, usually cold and highly excited, you work to get another rig together and lose it to a snag on the next cast—WOW!

Diversity is another long, sad story. Fisherman after fisherman gets into the habit of narrowing himself down to one or two types of terminal rig: "Oh, I use nothing but eggs!" How many times you hear a supposedly experienced fisherman say some variation of this kind of nonsense (personal prejudice again)! It just does not make sense to me to invest good money, time and effort into any endeavor, then cut the odds for success by narrowing the field from your side but not the other. Those fish are in their home—you are the interloper! With minor exceptions those fish are not residents of the water. They are just passing through. Everything is against you then, and you must be prepared to overcome these obstacles in order to turn those odds as much in your favor as possible. I have never known a consistently successful fisherman who didn't give preparation as one of the major reasons for his success. He could always list one more—diversity. Be prepared to offer those fish as many different attractions as possible.

I have experienced what I shall relate many times, but one special instance sticks in my mind. My partner and I hit two of our favorite drifts one morning, knowing from reports that the fish were in. The water was bordering on perfect. We egged and wormed for over an hour—nothing. . .deadsville. My partner came up to talk the situation over, and, while we discussed our misery, he popped a wobbler through the drift—wham! The story is that we both limited right there, side by side, from that one drift. Don't ask why the bait and drifters didn't work—I have no idea. The point is, we were on the verge of packing it in. Many fishermen would have done the same. As it was, we came away with two apiece on the bank and one nice, fat female to take home for the eggs and a delicious meal.

Just a word about checking your gear. I know it sounds silly to admonish any fisherman about checking his tackle from time to time, but let's fact it—we all forget. In the heat of a lost fish the tendency is to throw caution to the winds. "Get the gear into the water—fast. There's a twenty-pounder lying out there starving to death!" Wham! He's hooked, and then goodby because the leader had been frayed by the one just lost. Consternation—swear words—dire thoughts! Your fault, sucker—a simple run down the last three or four feet of line with thumb and forefinger might have saved both your partner's ears and the fish. That last section of line and the point of your hook must be checked constantly for wear and tear—it will pay off!

Correct, and correctly used, terminal tackle will make the difference between success and failure to any fisherman, but the importance lies in correct use. All of the very best of tackle available is squandered with poor practices at the drift. No one fisherman can get all the odds in his favor; he can only tip the scale his way so far with preparation. Then comes practice. The next chapter will discuss this and is, in my opinion, the center of the circle.

CHAPTER THREE

The Fish and the Water

The fish and the water—it's like the old tale about the chicken or the egg. I prefer the fish over the water, though—once the fish is understood, the water becomes easier to read and its mysteries begin to clear. Steelhead trout (and cutthroat), although anadromous, are quite different in actions and needs from salmon. Although these fish inhabit the same streams—often using the same water at the same time—their habits, ecology and biology are quite different. I will be discussing steelhead trout, in the main, but where a difference occurs I will try to show it within the context. Even within the races of steelhead trout (summer vs. winter) there lie basic differences in the actions and needs of the runs, and these must be understood to improve the success ratio.

Another factor stands out: "Generalization." There are seldom hard and fast rules in drift fishing, and this discussion will contain few, if any. Expound a hard rule, and the next fish will make you a liar. Most rules given here will run true

Fishing a tail-out type of drift on a small Oregon coastal stream.
— Photo by Leif Terdal

about 80 percent of the time though, and that's pretty fair odds. Personally I take the 80 percent and forget the 20 that's left. Considering fishing time, effort and all, I figure I just don't have any to spare for messing around on the low side of the scale.

Knowing the fish and the water is the old nitty-gritty, though. Five thousand dollars' worth of prime equipment won't land fish if you are on the stream at the wrong time or can't find what is there. I consider these areas of prime importance and would recommend that you do some outside reading on the subject. Two books come to mind that are definitive and beautifully written. They are *Fisherman's Fall* and *Return to the River,* both by Roderick Haig-Brown. They discuss steelhead and salmon in fresh water while on their spawning runs. These are great books for developing that "river-sense" which all successful fishermen need.

You will never reach the point, as a fisherman, where you know too much about the sport. Nor will you ever get beyond learning something new as each season passes. I guess this is a part of fishing that makes it endure with man—a kind of constant frontier. As you learn and grow you are very insensitive if you don't begin to form a deep attachment for your quarry. You know a "fisherman" the minute you begin to exchange ideas. He is immediately recognized on the banks of the stream, too. You also know the "scissorbill". A novice is not necessarily a scissorbill because this is a matter of attitude more than experience. A jerk is a jerk no matter how long he has been fishing or how many fish he takes home. I bring this up because anyone who takes up a sport and doesn't become a sportsman is to me a rather sad type. Understand, I'm not talking about the type of "sportsman" glorified in some of our sports media. If he doesn't have a guide or he can't afford to fly in 7,000 miles he's helpless. That's not my kind of sportsman.

My kind of sportsman is the man who is concerned. He loves his sport and will translate this into action to preserve and enhance the resource. I guess it boils down to a love of nature. With this comes a respect for your fellow fishermen, the fish, and the environment, that makes the word "sportsman" mean something.

Now, how about these beasties?

THE FISH

There are very few "wild" runs of steelhead trout left in the United States. Due mostly to the insane depredations of man, it has become necessary to artificially propagate these fish in order to preserve the runs. The salmon are following close behind. The Washington Department of Game pioneered this steelhead planting program, and the results have been spectacular. Oregon's Game Commission was slower but has also had tremendous success. Oregon has now embarked on a very solid series of experiments (on the Rogue River for one) and plantings that promise to spread these fish to areas either bereft, or poorly supplied with runs. They need and deserve luck and a great deal of public support. The chinook salmon presents a whole new ball game in artificial propagation and is, in my opinion, in trouble—especially the spring chinook. A shy fish—not easily hatchery raised, and extremely subject to loss from dams and other man-made

Indians dip net fishing at Celilo Falls on the Columbia before it was inundated in 1957 by the Dalles Dam. The Indians' fishing was capitalized for $27,000,000, which was then paid to four tribes. —Oregon Historical Society photo

Fishing for steelhead in January at the mouth of the Middle Fork of the Salmon River in Idaho. Notice the chunks of ice in the water! Steelhead and salmon are now in the process of fighting for their very existence in Idaho because of dams. — Photo by Bob Johnson

foolishness—the springer faces an enemy in every direction. The fact that Oregon still allows gill netting of all of these anadromous fish is an anachronism of monumental proportions. Why is it that 19th century management and harvest techniques still are followed in the 1970's? Could it possibly be greed? Read a book called *The Politics of Conservation* and learn what this greed did to Alaska prior to that territory's becoming a state. Then wise up, fishermen, before it's too late!

Artificial propagation starts with the taking of the eggs, but the critical time is when the fry reach the smolt stage. This is the time (the discovery of which provided the break-through in raising the return percentages) when the young fish go through changes signifying their physical readiness for downstream migration. Then starts the voyage that culminates with the return to spawn two, three or four years later.

Since all of the anadromous species I am talking about seek and need somewhat the same conditions, differing primarily by season, I will confine this section to winter steelhead trout, with asides for summer fish, and discuss the salmon later.

ANADROMOUS TROUT AND SALMON

CHINOOK SALMON

COHO SALMON

If end of upper jawbone extends beyond back of eye, your fish is a male.

STEELHEAD TROUT

SEA-RUN CUTTHROAT TROUT

STATE OF CALIFORNIA
DEPARTMENT OF FISH AND GAME

These fish begin to gather at the mouths of the rivers late in the fall, awaiting the freshet of rain that will call them upstream. Strays may be found in the streams as early as October, but the mass migration begins usually after Thanksgiving and continues on through the end of January. Weather becomes the key for both the fish and the fisherman.

The first rains of early fall have swept away the leaves and debris but not the mud. Now, with winter coming on and the rain becoming the rule rather than the exception, heavy water begins to flow. The river swirls where it was once dry and bounds where it once frolicked. Mud attends it, and we have a dirty brown, high, rolling torrent. The fish love it, and they pour past the bars through tidal basins and into the running stream. When the rain stops and the nights turn cold, the stream will drop and begin to clear. Here nature provided a boon: Each stream is different. Some are slow to muddy and fast to clear. As you explore and learn, you find the peculiarities of each stream providing knowledge of where to go under what conditions.

The best time is during the dropping and clearing of the water. Steelhead trout (and the other anadromous fish, too) are looking for two things constantly in their travel upstream: Rest and safety. Generally, the farther upstream the fish travels, the more rest he needs, and the distance between stops becomes shorter. During this rest the fish seeks safety. He is, after all, a wild animal and will utilize the natural configurations the stream provides to secure this. The longer he resides in fresh water and the closer he comes to his act of spawning, the more marked by his odyssey the fish becomes. Red begins to appear along

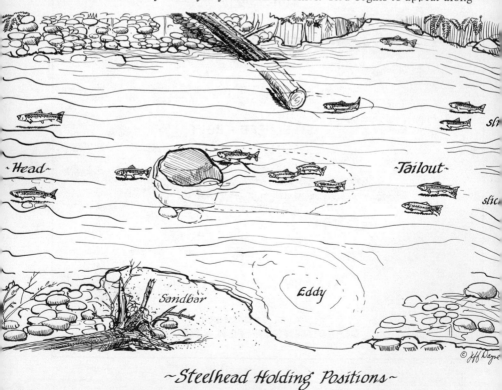

~Steelhead Holding Positions~

40

his sides; the bright silver gleam dulls to a poor gray, and the deep blue-black of the back loses its life and dulls to a grayish darkness. Spawning occurs, and the fish takes on a snake-like appearance, long and skinny. If he lives through the dangers, he will recover, begin to feed, and return to sea.

A fish in this condition is not fit for the table and demands release. The flesh is softened and the fat depleted. Truly, the fish is exhausted and is worthless to kill. The release of a dark or spawned-out fish is one mark of a sportsman. The old excuse, "Well, he's good enough to smoke," is beyond contempt. Scissorbills!

THE WATER

Ask any consistently successful fisherman what his secret is, and he'll most likely lie. The secret is: "First, know your water!"

In the foreward of this book I talked some about "shotgunning." If you wish to become consistent in your fishing success, then shotgunning is fatal. You must learn your water. Once you have settled on a stream and begun your quest for its fish, explore it. Take a mile or so as your area and walk it in late summer at the lowest water. Now you can see what the drifts look like without the guesswork of winter water conditions. You place the boulders and sunken logs, the cut banks and graveled runs in your memory.

HOLDING WATER

Steelhead trout like smooth, flowing water running from about three to twelve feet deep. The shape of a steelhead allows it to rest in water moving (to the eye)

slick

ead   Drift   Tailout

slick

Attain coverage by making short; successively longer casts...   Then move down and repeat the pattern...   Fish the entire drift.

© Jeff Dayne

~Typical Drift~

41

quite swiftly. Page 40 has a diagram of a typical section of steelhead holding water. This "drift" or "hold" will be the area that you must work when you fish. For purposes of clarity I'll label the top (upstream) end as the "head," the center section as the "drift" and that portion just above the lower end rapids as the "tailout". You will notice in the diagram I have shown fish to be spread generally throughout the drift. These fish will be using the natural protections provided to seek a safe rest. The diagram is an over-simplification, of course— you'll seldom be lucky enough to find a drift loaded like that. But the diagram does show you some of the areas within the drift where fish will normally be found. Remember that fish will use the same kind of area time after time—given similar water conditions. If action is produced in a certain area of a drift—mark it! Come back here again next trip or even later in the day on the same trip. Unless you're in a small pocket, you'll likely find more than one.

For summer fish the head of a drift will often be very productive. This is not as true for winter fish, but don't pass it up. In the summertime, as stream flows recede and oxygen becomes depleted, you'll often find the fish holding right in the riffles or boils at the head of the drift. Places you would expect to find resident trout will provide many a summer steelhead.

Winter fishing becomes most productive in the smooth parts of the drift— especially on larger streams. Small stream fishing for steelhead could fill a book on its own. Generally, you must remember that due to limitations of stream size, the fish will utilize every nook and cranny. The technique of fishing these pockets requires practice and patience to master, but is very rewarding.

Holding water can occur generally throughout a drift or it may be broken into sections. Steelhead are not partial to sand bottoms or roily water. These areas, although they often look inviting and will sometimes produce a fish, are not prime. Back eddies, too, do not provide the kind of water steelhead consistently use. The turbulent water directly behind a rock is also not a place for winter fish. A few feet downstream from these—where the water smooths—now we find him. A bait dropped in so as to provide the current opportunity to work it close by will cause the eruption you seek. Learn to read these currents. Watch the movement of your gear. You must be able to read, with accuracy, not only where the fish will be, but how to get your rig to them.

Let me digress a moment to make a point: No matter how many times you read this or have someone tell you about this, you must face the specter of trial and error. You are the only one who can provide this factor. It will teach you more than this or any other book. All I can do is provide the guidelines for you. Stream-side time is "on your own" fishing, for better or worse. So study your water before you cast. Try to figure out, as nearly as you can, what is going to happen to your gear from point A to point B.

THE TAILOUT

I give this section a special heading because it is so important. Generally, the fish will hold first in the tailout section of a drift before they move on. Also, fish will often drop back to this section during the time they spend in a drift. Summer fish love it and spend much of their time there. The tailout is that section directly above the riffle or rapids that empties the drift. It is prime.

Author Bill Luch tails a summer-run steelhead.

Study any tailout, and you will notice slicks occurring in the riffle below that provide easier passage to the fish. Directly above, or slightly to the side of these "V's" you will most often find your fish. Tailouts are usually shallow and sometimes difficult to fish. I'll discuss some techniques later. Tailout areas hold fish—that's the point to remember!

The major difference between winter and summer fish holding water is seasonal water conditions. The best hint I can give you is that in winter great sections of water can be passed by with little loss. In summer, never pass up an inch. Treat the summer steelhead as a resident—every rock and run may hold fish under, behind or within.

Again I'll say it—no one can teach you to read water. That skill will come from experience. I shudder to think of all the good water I passed by when I was beginning. But a fish here and one there started me learning my lessons.

Hopefully, what I say here will give you at least a head start. Streamside time is still the greatest teacher, however.

Reading water is an art. You simply cannot learn the subtleties of currents or holding areas by reading about them. I suppose I should not be setting that kind of information down on paper—it's kind of author's sacrilege. But there is no use misleading anyone, and I certainly won't attempt to. The beginner is between a rock and a hard place and will just have to work his way out. Perhaps I shall be able to get a couple of hints across that will help you learn, but don't expect more.

Most of your learning will come by returning to the same stretch of water several times. As you cast and drift through, patterns will take shape in a drift that will remain with you from trip to trip. Believe me when I tell you that herein lies your beginning success at drift fishing. Current patterns are the same, really. When water flows over a submerged boulder, it causes a boil. When water breaks around and above surface rock, it eddies close behind and forms a miniature drift for the next ten to fifteen feet—depending on the size of the rock. You will find that slowly you'll begin to know just where to drop your bait to get a drift from behind the rock, rather than just having a straight drop, then a snag.

Every foot of a drift has its own pattern. Although several trips may be spent finding the key to this pattern on your drift or drifts—after practical experience it comes quickly. You will find that, after awhile, one or two casts will give you this pattern. Indeed, you will have a good idea of the pattern before you even start to cast.

What, exactly, is this pattern I am talking about? Every time you cast, your sinker should travel through the drift in a rather modified arc. (See page 41.) The first part of your drift will be more or less straight downstream. Then, as the limits of your line are reached, the sinker will start bending across current toward you, ending up more or less straight away downstream. This is the first part of the pattern—the arc of the drift. The second part is the bottom. Your gear, as it works through the drift, will encounter all of the peculiarities of the bottom along the arc. By sight and feel you can begin to understand this part of your drift. You will feel the action of the sinker and, by watching where your line is traveling, will be able to pick out some of the objects that cause this feel. You won't get them all, but will get enough so that you'll begin to know when to lift the rod to miss a boulder and when to lower it to allow your gear to drop into a depression, etc.

As you widen your capabilities, you will naturally begin to widen your fishing area. Oh, you'll still get fooled now and then, but, if you've learned your lessons, not more than once on any section of a drift. There are those fishermen that are just naturals. These lucky souls walk into a strange drift with strange or new gear and, presto! The drift and all that it holds is theirs. I was never this lucky—all that I learned came by constant fishing and snag after snag.

SNAGS

Any discussion of water could never be complete without a discussion of snags. Fishing, as you must, in close contact with the bottom, you are going to get snags. The point is academic. It's what you do with them that matters. Many snags will release quite easily; three or four sharp pulls on the rod will lift them loose. Sometimes, if the snag is downstream of you, slacking the line down

Archie Herron (left) and Dale Quackenbush compare their steelhead. — Photo by Hank Bottemiller

so that a belly forms in the line downstream of the snag will allow the current to pull you loose. Once in a while a slow, steady pull will cause the sinker to slip or break off and save the rig. It boils down to the amount of time you spend on them. I have actually seen "fishermen" fool with a snagged rig for five or ten minutes. This is ridiculous. At the most, your rig is worth fifty cents. The very thought that any man would stand around for ten minutes snapping his line up and around and make the water sizzle and swish trying to overturn a hundred-pound boulder is beyond belief. Aside from the fact that his economics are severely twisted, look what he is doing to the drift. Then you have the idiot in waders who wades halfway across the river (into the water holding fish) to free his ten-cent egg rig by sticking the tip of his rod down and fishing around through the rocks. That man doesn't need fishing therapy—he belongs on a couch at $50 an hour. For heaven's sake, friends, if three or four sharp lifts on the rod won't free your gear, point the rod at the snag, hold onto the line, and back off. The snag will give, or your gear will; at any rate, you can get back to fishing again.

WATER HEIGHT AND CLARITY

I can't tell you much about water height that will help you—it depends on the stream you are fishing. If the water is too high, you will have great trouble getting a drift; too low and you face spooky fish. Clarity is another thing. As the water drops, it will clear. Again, know your stream for there are streams in the Northwest that will clear in twelve hours or less.

Once you are able to see your bait or lure in two or three feet of water, the stream is very fishable. Most winter fishermen like to see the stream with a green tinge. This is the water fish seem to love to travel in, and usually marks the "good" fishing days. As winter deepens you will face frozen conditions and with them, low, clear water. Most of the fish stop moving and hold in the drifts. They also become much more wary and spooky. The fishing calls for caution in your approach, and many times a cast must be made well back from the edge of the water. Here is another reason for a beginner to start on a larger stream. The very size of the river will negate some of this low water factor and make experience less of a factor in taking fish under these conditions. During these low water times look to the tailout.

I'll leave this subject by repeating something I said previously: You are invading the fishes' home ground. As with any invader you have the disadvantages mostly on your side. Approach the problem casually, and you will have casual success. Study the problem and reason out the difficulties, and you will begin to win—consistently. There's a great deal of pleasure in winning. There is also a great deal of pleasure in figuring out how to win. Above all, be a "fisherman," not a "scissorbill". The stream belongs to all, of course, but the drift belongs to the man who is there first. A simple, "Hi! Do you think there's room for two?" will establish your credentials faster than ten fish in ten casts. Courtesy and consideration to your fellow fishermen is a mark of quality. Some call it "class".

CHAPTER FOUR

Drift Fishing Technique

A bove you will find a pretentious title for "hints". I say this because no two fishermen are alike. The rules of water, where the fish are, etc., are the same for all of us—not so the techniques. We each develop our own little quirks for getting the job done. Over the years these are modified, changed, discarded, etc. My partne⁻, Jim Regan, and I have fished together for many years. Trip after trip we fish the water together, taking fish, losing fish, missing fish, each with our own style. We read the water the same ways; we agree on where the fish will be, but we have our own ways of going after them. What I am trying to say is that in the final analysis, your style, if it gets you fish consistently, is (or will be) correct for you. If it works for you, you'll be a fool to change.

There are techniques, though, that will help the beginner. These guidelines are what I shall discuss here. Try them. If they help you—great! If you can refine them or change them to help you more—that's great, too!

CASTING

Overtly, the cast is simply the act of propelling your gear from where you are to the beginning point of your drift. There's more to it than that. How about the brush behind you, the overhanging tree across from you, the big rock in front of you? Where are the fish? Can I get my gear to them from where I'm standing? Where will my gear drift to if I cast from here and it lands over there? Each cast has these questions attached. They can only be answered on the stream bank. Some points can be studied here, however.

Since you want your gear to travel through the drift maintaining close contact with the bottom, you must cast correctly to insure this happening. Most beginning fishermen cast overhand. This seems to be a natural action for casting and is easily picked up by the beginner. The trouble that is encountered is too much arc to the gear in flight, incorrect release of the line (usually at too high a position in the forward thrust of the rod), causing the gear to travel high in the air on its way out. There are, of course, many times when you can get away with this kind of a cast. But a high-arc cast is a poor cast for drift fishing for three reasons: It is seldom accurate; the chance of confrontation with an overhanging tree is always present; far too much slack occurs in the line after the rig hits the water due to that high arc.

There are times when an overhand (and sometimes two-handed) cast will be a necessity. On a large river where maximum distance is needed, you must get all the rod's backbone behind the cast, and this is the way to do it. Most drift fishing casts can be made without these three drawbacks. Try casting sidearm. This type of cast is not as natural to most people and takes a little learning. Several advantages are realized, however: Reduced worry about brush, etc., to your rear, better pin-point accuracy, almost immediate control over your gear due to less arc. By bringing the rod tip up during its forward travel, some arc can be created in order to achieve greater distance.

Accuracy is what you must strive for. Practice is the only thing that will provide this for you. It will come down to learning when to release the line during the forward movement of your rod. A cast may be shortened or stopped by laying the forefinger alongside of, and just in front of, the spool of your reel during the last few feet of travel. The line coming off the spool will hit your finger and be slowed or stopped. An over-exhuberant cast after a strike can be prevented from landing in the brush by this method.

Pin-point accuracy is every fisherman's desire, of course, but few of us really achieve this perfection. Two or three feet from your point of aim will do very nicely for the majority of casts. If you can get down to three out of four in the one- to two-foot range, you are doing very well, indeed. I might add that practice with just a weight on the end of your line is not good enough. If you feel practice is necessary, such as casting to an innertube, use a full rig. The casting of a full rig is quite different in action and technique than with just a weight. Primarily, what you are learning is the feel of the combination of your rod, size of reel spool, weight of line and type of gear. This combination, once you become familiar with it, will tell you how hard to whip the rod through and when to release the line from your forefinger.

Placing yourself on the bank of the stream facing your target presents another immediate problem: How do you cast so that your gear begins to work for you immediately upon reaching your target area? To effect this you must quarter your cast upstream. Quartering does not mean casting one-fourth of the distance upstream above your target. It means laying your gear far enough above, straight away from you, so that, considering current action and sinker weight, your gear will be on bottom and working when it arrives at a position straight out from you. The amount of quartering will vary. Too much is the biggest worry. This causes extra slack to occur and will result in more snags. Provide just enough distance above straightaway to allow your gear to settle and go to work.

There will be a certain amount of slack resulting from this, and it must be taken up. Sometimes lifting the tip of the rod will remove it—more often a crank or two on the reel will be called for. Some slack is necessary to allow the gear to sink to the bottom, so not all need be removed. What you must attempt is to balance the slack necessary to reach bottom quickly with the need for a fairly tight line. If you allow too much line to accumulate, a belly will result.

Bellied line is caused by the current ahead of the gear. This downstream belly must be avoided. It makes it impossible to follow your gear by eye. A belly will also remove the "feel" of your gear. Remove that "feel" and you remove your chances of taking fish. A large belly in the line also provides for snags. Allowing

The head of a male steelhead with kype on lower jaw.
— Photo by Eric Carlisle

the gear to stop without your knowing it, the belly prevents you from quickly lifting off or over the snag. The sinker or rig has a chance to settle in, and you're done. Properly handled, the line, at its juncture with the water, must be close to straight on with the sinker. As stated, not all of the belly can be removed. The fisherman must strive, on each cast, to take out enough to retain his "feel" while allowing a bottom-bumping drift to occur.

THE DRIFT

Over and over you have read "on the bottom" repeated in the text. Steelhead trout, chinook, coho and cutthroat trout (to a lesser degree) are bottom dwellers. When these fish rest, they do so in that portion of the water from bottom gravel up to about 14 inches or so. Unless your gear is presented to them during the drift in their area, very little success will be achieved. You'll hear the stories about the eggs taken while skittering across the top of the water, or the lure grabbed at the feet during retrieve—wonderful! Some of them may even be true. Once I had a winter steelhead take my eggs on top of the water, too—once! Summer fish will hit a dry fly from time to time.

Just the other day I took a break from writing this epic and made a trip to a nearby stream for summer fishing. While enjoying the sun on the water (after the early morning fishing was over), I saw a nice bright summer-run take a large moth fluttering on the water in a long pool. The moth fell, the water boiled— no more moth. Winter fish and salmon? Well, you go ahead and fish high—I'll

49

follow you—gladly! Cutthroat, too, love a fly and will rise. Nevertheless, the bottom 14 inches or so of river will produce ten to one.

All species will follow a lure—some more readily than others. Most—if they haven't struck in the first three of four feet of following—will not do so. The coho salmon and cutthroat trout will follow a lure quite readily in certain types of water. A spinner or wobbler (spinner and worms for cutthroat) if fished up through a long pool will take these fish quite consistently! This is not drift fishing, however, and as far as I am concerned, drift fishing beats this cast and retrieve method any day. There are, however, stretches of water simply not conducive to drifting; then it's "any port in a storm."

So—you have the right size sinker and you've cast correctly—now what? You must attempt to get that rig through the drift to entice the fish to pick it up. I have been asked many times at steelhead clinics put on by the Northwest Steelheaders, "How often should my gear hit the bottom?" The answer is, of course, often enough to keep your bait 14 inches or so from the bottom. How often will depend on the kind of bottom and the current you face. Steelhead will answer a fairly fast drift of the gear; salmon like their bait to be traveling more slowly. I like to know that I am hitting bottom at least every two or three feet during a drift. If I am using a floating type of lure (Corky, etc.), I like a closer contact than this if I can get it without hanging up. On a good, small-gravel bottom, you can sometimes get down to a rolling of the sinker as it travels—perfection! That situation doesn't occur often, though.

As your gear travels it will stop from time to time—usually because a larger rock has hung the sinker. Most times, if you haven't allowed a belly to develop, one crank on the reel, or a slight lift of the rod tip, will free your gear. If this doesn't happen a sharp raise of the rod is needed fast to prevent the sinker from becoming securely lodged. Once free, slack off quickly to allow that sinker to get back to its job.

INCREASING DRIFT DISTANCE

Often, about one-half the way through your arc of drift, current action against your gear will begin to pick your rig away from the bottom. This point is normally reached just about the time your gear arrives at the limit of its downstream travel and begins to move across current back toward you. You can increase the downstream travel of your gear by beginning an operation called "tailing" right at this point. Tailing is the act of backing off with your reel to allow the gear to continue traveling downstream. Some fishermen open the bail of their reel and allow line to peel off—controlling the amount with their forefinger on the spool. The former method is the better one, though, because it provides for a great deal more control. By careful reverse action of the reel, pausing often to continue to feel bottom, a drift can be significantly increased. Often you will find yourself on a drift literally stuck by lack of access in one spot—brush upstream and down and water too deep to wade. Learning the technique of tailing will be invaluable so that you can cover water you would otherwise not be able to reach. Many an otherwise unfishable tailout can be reached by tailing down to it along the far bank, then working the gear back across in your dirction. The success of tailing will depend on starting just prior to the gear's beginning to travel across the current, keeping close control over the amount of line released so that the line doesn't get ahead of the sinker, so that when tailing begins the current will keep your gear moving in the direction of the area you want to reach. Cover the water—that's the answer. Tailing is one help to you in your attempt.

FISHING THE TAILOUT

Prior to this I have talked about the tailout of the drift. It is prime holding water. One of its drawbacks, however, is the fact that it is usually fairly shallow and hard to drift. Many tailout areas are literally impossible to fish in the normal downstream drift. Learn to cross-current your drift to make up for these difficulties. Page 41 shows you a diagram with one cast running downstream and across to a point just above or alongside a tailout. By working your gear (alternately raising and lowering your rod), you can bring about a crossing of your bait or lure—directly across the face of the fish. By starting fairly high and increasing your cast each time, you can cover the tailout all the way down to where the current breaks over into the rapids. The current of a tailout will be as fast or faster than the main section of the drift, but will not usually exert as much drag on your gear because of the lesser depth. Given this lessened pull, you will find that you have to "work" your way across the current—often to your sudden gain. Many times you will come to a point where you just can't get your gear to move any more. Try working the gear back toward you—*slowly*. Just a wind or two at a time with a pause between will often entice a fish to pick up the bait. Don't try this with a weighted lure! But a flatfish-type lure is deadly in these waters and works very well when used to fish a tailout.

If you happen to be lucky enough to find a drift where you can get out far enough into the river to work more or less straight away downstream, you can "sweep" the tailout. By extending your casts a yard or so at a time, starting from first one side and then the other, a tailout can be worked or swept. The effect is very productive once you get the hang of it.

THE BITE

Summer steelhead are feeders. As such they are much more aggressive in their actions, and when they bite you are usually very aware of it. Most provide a hard rap, rap, rap on the lure or bait that is unmistakably *fish!*

Now the hard part: Winter steelhead and salmon are not feeders. They seldom strike. Often they don't even bite as most fishermen think of fish biting. Winter steelhead are the epitome of this type of action. Mouthing the bait is their favorite trick. These fish can stop a bait, mouth it and spit it out again so softly that most untuned fishermen never realize what has happened. There is no given, provable ratio of the number of rocks that stop your gear to the number of fish. Heaven knows there are vastly more rocks. Some of those stops are fish, though. How do you know for sure?

Let's consider some of the things that happen during a drift. (I admit to over-simplification, but allow me that as literary license.)

1. You have made three or four casts through a drift, all within one or two feet of each other. Each cast has gone through what feels like a small-rock bottom, no stops, no snags. Cast number five and halfway through your gear stops.

2. You are on your fourth cast through the same water. The sinker is bumping along what feels to you like every two feet or so—suddenly the bump quickens to every six inches.

3. Your gear has stopped and when you lifted the rod to free it, the rock moved.

4. You are drifting through with a nice, tight line and suddenly you notice a belly appearing—how did that occur?

Simple sounding, I agree. But laugh if you want; I have stood alongside fishermen and watched these things occur while they were totally unaware of what their gear was doing. Set the hook! In each of the above, the odds are at least even that it's a fish. Make each of these less exact, less simple and the factors more real and you begin to see why so many fish are missed. You can get by with haywired gear, sloppy casts and dull hooks, but fail to learn how to recognize the bite, and you lose!

I can only tell you some things to look for—things to be aware of. Look for a break in symmetry or rhythm. Each drift has its own rhythm. Several casts and drifts through will begin to impart to your senses this rhythm. It is not a constant one because there are variations of bottom and depth and current, but it is a thing that can be sensed. When this is broken in a new or different way, set the hook! If you suddenly find a snag that wasn't there the last three casts, set the hook! A belly cannot occur in a tight line, even if you do snag up, unless you are letting out line. A fish picking up your bait and moving upstream will cause one, through. Set the hook!

Many times a fish will pick up the lure or bait and drift back with it as it moves through the water. That fish may pull the sinker free from bottom. Now, if you have gone through this drift with good bottom contact before and nothing has happened to make you lose a sinker, set the hook! It is impossible to cover all the quirks of this subtle action. The realm of possibilities is too vast. There aren't really any rules, either, except perhaps that of concentration. A lapse in concentration loses many a fish. The time to talk, joke or light up or warm hands or any of those things man just has to do when fishing is when the gear is out of the water. If you go fishing to hook fish (why drive fifty miles to talk to your neighbor?), then when that gear is working you should be working. The punch won't be telegraphed and always comes when not expected. Be ready!

I realize that this sort of lecturing sounds fatuous. I don't mean it to be, but I make no apologies. I've seen what I have just described happen too many times. It's rather sad to watch a man miss fish simply because he's not paying attention. I don't really mind if he's a stranger, and I'm waiting to follow him on the drift. Ordinarily, it doesn't pay to follow anyone on a drift—but that poor soul won't bother anything. Nine chances out of ten if you said to him, "Hell, man, set your hook; there's a fish out there!" he'd say, "Huh?"

Cutthroat trout bite like trout—'nuff said. Chinook and winter steelhead are real softies and must be closely attended. Coho are more bold and usually let you know they're around. Summer steelhead are not a bit shy about biting, and you become very aware of them, very fast. There it is in capsule form—watch what you're doing and feel what's happening (or not happening) out there—set the hook!

Wallace Bergerson with a hefty Nehalem River steelhead that fell for a bobber-type steelhead drift fishing lure. — Photo by Frank W. Amato

SETTING THE HOOK

Just a word about this business of setting a hook. All of these fish have a bony ridge around the outer edge of the mouth. Don't hesitate to sock it to 'em! You won't break an unflawed line on a good, solid set. So don't be half-hearted—when you think it's a fish, give it a good solid shot. You'll see the "fisherman" who sets at every pause during the drift. The only thing I can say here is more power to him—his arm will need it by the end of the day! This practice doesn't need to be followed by anyone. If you concentrate on what's happening to your gear, you will be able to pick out the difference between rock and fish at least 80 percent of the time. It comes down to the fish's being alive and the rock certainly not. Even though the fish may not "jerk" on the gear, he certainly has some movement. With the right tackle and concentration, you will feel that movement, no matter how slight.

WORKING THE GEAR

You must have figured out by now that drift fishing consists of a great deal more than just tossing out the bait and letting the current do the rest. The gear must be "worked" through the drift. The better the job you learn to do at this, the higher your success.

Start your learning correctly. Certain bad habits should never be given a chance to catch on. When you begin to fish a drift, start by setting the anti-reverse of your reel to "off". This should be kept in the "off" position while fishing except during the time you are actually fighting a fish. Keep one hand on that reel handle so that you are instantly ready to pick up, or back off, on your gear. An instantaneous response will prevent many a snag. Add to this the ready ability to "tail" by backing off on your reel so as to reach more water. Many times a slight pick up at the reel when the gear has paused will remove just enough excess slack to allow you to feel the "thrumming" or very slight "surge" that translates into *"fish"*!

The gear must be constantly "worked" through the drift. The rod is lifted or lowered, the reel used to pick up or back off. All of these actions go toward the "feel" of the drift. Sometimes your gear will travel to a part of the drift where the shallowness of the water or a slackening of the current will stop further drifting. Often these areas may be fished quite effectively by slowly retrieving line, pausing as you do so to allow the bait to settle. For some reason worms work well in this type of situation. Tailout sections of the drift are often the type of water that must be fished this way. There is a drift I know of on a close-to-Portland stream that has to be worked in this manner; it seldom fails to produce at least one fish. The water at the end of the drift makes a sharp right-angle turn. This angle has created a deeper pool just beyond the turn that has a lighter current through it. By casting across and down, the bait (weighted lures won't work here) can be worked down into the back of this pool. The current isn't strong enough to carry the sinker along so you must retrieve, stop—retrieve, stop—or "work" your gear through, until the main current catches it and carries it away. The fish coming up the chute love this area and hold here before moving on into the drift. Casting directly into the pocket seems to spook the fish, but "working" into the same area from above seldom fails to produce. There are many areas like this, and the technique of "working" the gear is invaluable.

Weighted lures (spinners and wobblers) must also be "worked" but in a different manner. Fish the above-mentioned water with a weighted lure, and the results will be—snag! Working a weighted lure consists mostly of keeping all slack out of the line thus reducing the chances of a snag. On most larger streams a weighted lure will require a small amount of extra weight to keep it on the bottom. The difference between this and bait is the factor of the weight of the lure. Even the slightest amount of hesitation at the sinker will allow the lure to begin to find a rock to roll under. Because of this, some pressure must be constantly applied to minimize this trouble. Understand now, this pressure is not applied in order to keep the lure working—the current will take care of this very well. You work the lure this way simply to control the lure better, remove slack and lessen the possibility of snags. Because of this pressure, however, you usually don't get as long a drift with a weighted lure as with bait, etc. This doesn't translate into a drawback, though, as lures may be fished by casting upstream, across or angling downstream, so the water may be covered just as efficiently.

A flatfish-type of lure is great for sweeping the tailout or working through a drift. Since the lure floats, you have less worry about snagging—only the sinker need be considered. This factor allows this type of lure to be worked like bait. The difference is that the lure will have action and, thus, extra attractiveness. Let me repeat: The current will provide all the action a lure needs through a drift—the spinner does not have to be spinning at top speed to do its job!

COVERING A DRIFT

Personally, I like to start fishing a new drift (new to me, that is) at the tailout and work my way upstream. (I start on familiar water in the area that has provided fish on previous trips.) The tailout is where the fish first stop as they come into the drift. Then, as you work upstream, you are approaching the fish from behind, and, especially in low water, that is an important factor. Cover the water completely. By this I mean fish the close water first and work out and away from you. If the drift is a good one (no shallowing or slack areas), I move only a few yards at a time as I work upstream. The object is to cover all the water as thoroughly as possible. In low, clear water, very cold water, or water that has high color, the fish won't move far to pick up your gear. The bait or lure must be presented right to the fish in order to entice him into action.

A point needs to be made here. Often in low, clear water, you can see your fish. Under all but the most special circumstances this is not good. In eight out of ten cases when you see the fish they have seen you first. This will usually be the end of fishing for those particular fish. During the summer or during low winter water, a cautious approach must be used. Stay as far from the water as possible; stay behind the fish, and stay quiet. During the "nightcrawler incident" I mentioned in an earlier chapter, some jerk ran right out into the drift below me when he saw me hook a fish.

The crazy thing about this was that the waist-deep water he crashed into was right where I had ended my drift and hooked the fish! "Old Crasher," as my partner and I began calling him, promptly cast across the stream into the berry vines. That jerk stood there waist deep in the fishing water and jerked on that berry vine for five minutes before finally wading ashore and breaking off. Weird? Just wait.

I had to get away from him at all costs, so I took off downstream to the next drift. Luckily, I crossed the stream, and the drift could be fished from my side only. My partner dropped on down to the next water below. Now "Old Crasher" was across from me and couldn't fish my drift—look out, partner! Down he went to the next drift, but he was blocked by a sheer wall. Splash, splash, splash, across the riffle he came at a dead run. Just behind my partner was a pool about six feet deep. In went that fool at a dead run. My partner and I laughed, but it wasn't really funny—it was pathetic and disgusting. Here's the funny part: Two or three hours later, when we returned downstream on our way home, there was "Old Crasher" standing in the middle of the drift he had spooked first off—still casting at the berry vines across the way—wonderful! I am not writing this to tell funny stories, however, and I hope to make a point, however broadly drawn. I have seen far too many fishermen standing in water that has produced fish to not mention this story. It's idiotic.

NEW METHODS AND TACKLE

Although corking is not new to steelhead fishing, having been used in Canada (particularly southern British Columbia) for years, it is relatively new to most of us in the States. Designed to use a floating device to aid in fishing snaggy waters, corking may be utilized on any river with excellent results.

The object is to set up your gear in such a way as to be able to use a cork but have enough line between the cork and the sinker so as to be on the bottom.

Again terminal tackle remains the same. On the main line tie a blocking snell (many fishermen use a rubber band) that will stop the cork but pass through the guides of the rod. The block must be as tight as possible to prevent movement by any other means than being pulled up or down the line to adjust for the depth of the stream. The cork is placed between the block and the swivel that connects the main line with the leader and is fixed so that it slides freely between the block and the swivel. Now when the cast is made the line can be reeled all the way in, then be allowed to run free as the sinker drops to the bottom and the corks hits the stopper. The necessity here is to find out the depth of the water so as to place the stopper the proper distance up the line.

I have had good luck with making up my own corks. I glue two wine corks together end to end with epoxy, paint one end fluorescent red or orange for visibility and drill a hole through the center lengthways using a heated wire as my drill. This hole must be large enough in diameter to allow the line to run freely but small enough so that the stopper cannot get through.

By corking you can effectively fish those long, slow holes that you could never fish effectively before. You set the stopper so that the sinker is just ticking bottom from time to time, causing the cork to bob as it proceeds through the drift. If you have adjusted the stopper correctly, when the cork disappears—look out!

New tackle can be covered with one word: graphite. The newest thing to hit the fishing market, graphite is the cause of much discussion and argument, par-

Twenty-one pound Seymour River buck taken on a shrimp by Jim Mayers. — Photo by Eric Carlisle

ticularly with the fly rodders. You will see terms such as **HMG** or **LMG** when graphite is referred to in ads. These refer to high or low "modulus". All graphite has a high modulus of elasticity when compared to fiberglass. Being brittle, however, some graphite has added to it glass fibers to provide more flex and breaking strength. Bypassing all the jargon, graphite rods come down to a blending of graphite material (developed from space technology) and fiberglass material to provide a rod that has an incredible strength-to-size ratio. The new graphite rods will amaze you with their strength in relation to their small butt diameter.

Graphite rods have another feature that is important—recovery time speed. The graphite rods have the quality of super-fast flex recovery. In other words, they are very fast to return to a still position after being strongly flexed or bent. Many fly fishermen complain that this feature is unnerving and practically forces them to learn to cast all over again. However, with a drift rod this feature is all plus and will add to the rod no matter who is casting because a fast return to normal aids in line control (and backlash control for the casting reel fisherman).

More and more tackle companies are getting on the graphite bandwagon, but as far as I know there are no drift rods on the market as of this writing. Several companies are in the process of graphite drift rod marketing: Shakespear, Fenwick, to mention just a couple. One company here in the northwest, Lamiglass Corp., is very close to marketing a graphite drift rod. Lamiglass has been making

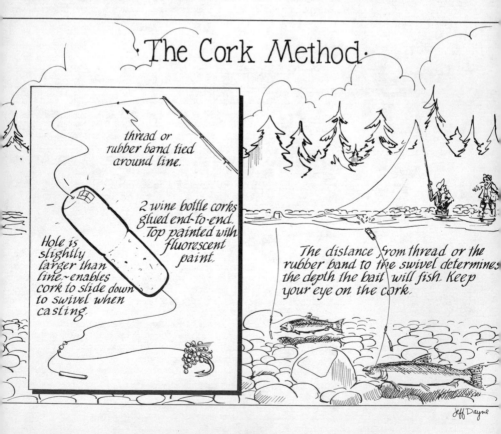

The Cork Method·

thread or rubber band tied around line.

2 wine bottle corks glued end-to-end. Top painted with fluorescent paint.

Hole is slightly larger than line~enables cork to slide down to swivel when casting.

The distance from thread or the rubber band to the swivel determines the depth the bait will fish. Keep your eye on the cork.

Jeff Dayne

glass blanks for a variety of rod makers for years and is finally putting their name on rods of their own manufacture. I have fished their new graphite drift rod, and it is great. Considering the quality of the drift rod, I would say the fly rod would be a dandy, too, although I haven't tried one. I have, however, fished with the Cortland graphite fly rod, and it was really a pleasure to use. (Lamiglass makes the blanks.)

The one drawback to graphite is its cost. Graphite material runs around $500 per pound, so that rods are costly. I think that time and mass marketing will lower these costs some, though. So, if you want a rod that is super-strong for size and has extremely fast recovery action, all you need to do is convince yourself and your checkbook keeper that the graphite rod (regardless of cost) is absolutely essential to your well-being, peace of mind, and continued good health—good luck!

CHAPTER FIVE

Salmon and Sea-Run Cutthroat Trout

Stream fishing for salmon is really not much different than for steelhead trout. The time of year is not the same, of course, but the technique is the same with some minor variations. I say "minor variations" and, indeed, they appear to be minor, but they will spell the difference between success and failure.

Drift fishing is the type of fishing I am talking about here. The other methods (trolling, lure casting, plunking) take many fish for anglers in the Pacific Northwest, but drifting is, in my opinion, more fun and can be more productive as well.

Chinook salmon are a very shy fish, especially the spring run. They often school up—even in fresh water—and will remain more or less together as they ascend their spawning stream. According to Haig-Brown, these fish do not move around a great deal within the pools. Indeed, he states that they are shy and very wary—easily disturbed and quick to spook. When the spring chinook begin to move into the tributaries of the Columbia, Willamette or other rivers flowing directly into the ocean, they are largely ignored by the drift fishermen. The months of May, June and even part of July can provide some excellent fishing for the drifter with a little effort and research. The Oregon and California game commissions and the Washington Department of Fisheries can supply you with information on runs of these fish as to timing, areas and size (numbers).

Salmon will usually hold in either the tailout or the deeper pool section of the drift. Not until they begin to spawn do you find them in the riffles in any numbers. By this time they are beyond providing any sport for the fisherman. All of the gear mentioned earlier in the text will take salmon—even worms. Eggs are by far the best, though, and probably provide more drift-caught salmon than any other bait. Spinners, wobblers and other lures work well when fished correctly. These may be drifted or the cast and retrieve method used, depending on the water. Long, deep, slow pools are ideal for casting and retrieving a lure. Fish them deep and slow! With bait, salmon respond better to a slow drift and a larger bait. A gob of eggs twice the size you would normally use for steelhead will be preferred by salmon. Drift your bait through as slowly as you can. This is tough to do because of snags but should be attempted. More sinker is called for as is more "working" of the gear. The bite is most often a very gentle tug, and it usually pays to allow a little time before the set to make sure the bait is well taken.

A good soft line of up to fifteen-pound test is called for with these fish. I personally fish spring salmon with twelve-pound test and have found it to be very satisfactory. The terminal rigs are much the same as for steelhead.

Fall chinook and coho ascend their home rivers from August through December. These runs are generally larger and more widespread than the spring run. Coho, as I have stated, are a much bolder fish. Haig-Brown comments on the repeated breaking off from the schools of individual coho and their moving all through the drift as if they were exploring. Coho bite with much more authority than do chinook, also with more fearlessness. They are not a very shy fish when it comes to responding to bait or lure. Also, coho will answer a faster drift than will chinook in most cases. Coho have one other rather wild habit: when you are fishing a long, deep area by casting and retrieving hardware, the coho will often follow the lure almost to the point when you lift it from the water before strinking. This can be very unnerving.

CUTTHROAT TROUT

Sea-run cutthroat are, in my judgment, a magnificent fish. They hit readily, fight very hard and are prime table fare. From August through December these fish provide an excellent and exciting fishery throughout the Northwest. The Washington Department of Game has, for some time, been planting these trout in the spring in many streams. Originally this was done to test the theory that those fish going un-caught during the regular trout season would migrate to sea and return as a sea-run to provide a double benefit. The information I have received is that the theory proved to be a good one—in effect, two fisheries for one. This has to be considered forward thinking and innovative fishery management

Bright, 23-pound spring chinook salmon taken while drift fishing with eggs. — Photo by Frank W. Amato

Clayton Hood holds a salmon by the tail while he un-hooks his spinner.

and, over the long haul, a very solid economic saving in a time of ever-increasing management costs.

Sometime in August, each year, these fish enter their spawning streams. After feeding in tidewater for a time they begin their journey into the fast waters of the river. Cutthroat will use the waters much as will the summer steelhead. Both are members of the trout family and both seem to take up residence in the stream. The main condition you face is low, clear water. Your approach to the water, then, is of primary importance. Cutthroat will respond to almost any bait or lure. Eggs, however, are pretty far down the preference list. Worms, crayfish tails, spinner and bait combinations, shrimp—all of these head the list, along with flies.

Again the difference is the water condition. Many times the smaller streams will be but a trickle in August, if you compare them with winter conditions. Lighter gear is called for, and a midge rod with two to four pound test line on a micro reel can be a joy to work with. I have a little seven-foot ultra-light magnum (I built it myself) that is supreme for these fish. A small tandem spinner with a worm dangling four to six inches behind, worked up through a long pool is an excellent way to fish these trout in low water.

Haig-Brown notes that cutthroat establish an area for themselves in their stream. From here they move forth to feed or fend off interlopers. This area must provide them with both a source of food (current flow to the area) and protection. The rule: Don't pass over any water. No matter how inhospitable it may look to you, if it meets the above criteria it could hold cutthroat. The broken water of a riffle, if it is at least a foot deep, will provide these conditions.

One more point: These fish remain in good condition through December. Chinook, coho, steelhead, all of these cross the runs of cutthroat. On those beautiful fall days a rich variety of enjoyment is yours by taking along some cutthroat gear. After a morning of chasing salmon through the heavier water, try switching to a light outfit and trying the riffles for them.

Fall chinook salmon from the Trask River, Oregon. These fifteen to twenty-pound salmon were taken on eggs. —Photo by Frank W. Amato

Author Bill Luch treats his wife, Virginia,
to some white water on the Deschutes.

CHAPTER SIX

Drift Boating for Steelhead

For many the first trip in a drift boat becomes the forerunner of a hobby that will stay with them until age makes it no longer possible to continue. Boating on a swift falling river can contain just about all a person wants in outdoor activities: Peaceful setting, contentment, beautiful scenery, excitement—you name it. In this section I will discuss the various kinds of boats and some hints concerning operation.

DRIFT BOATS

When drift boats first began to evolve (and they are a product of Oregon rivers) by combining design factors necessary to the rivers of Oregon and some of the features of New England row boats, they were named for the rivers of their use—McKenzie or Rogue. Today this differentiation has changed, and design factors have blurred and standardized. Generally you now have two main types of drift boats on the market. The McKenzie or Rogue boat (depending largely upon who is doing the calling) and the Rapid Robert. Don't ask me why.

Although these boat types are named differently, the techniques of operation are largely the same. Also, the safety rules are identical. With a McKenzie boat the sharp bow is pointed downstream during travel; with the Rapid Robert the bow is pointed upstream during travel. Fewer and fewer of the broad, high-sterned Rapid Roberts are seen today, although there is an outfit in the Puget Sound area building a modification of this hull from aluminum.

EVALUATING YOUR BOAT

The principle of a drift boat is the ability to drift downstream through fast, rough water and stay both upright and dry. Of course, some of this will depend largely upon the skill of the oarsman, but much is traceable to boat design. Here are some of the design factors you should check *before* you buy:

1. Bottom width is directly related to stability. Compare three or four different makers' specifications.

2. Flair width, i.e., width at top of sides. How much flair is there? This relates both to stability and interior dryness. Flair is the difference between bottom measure and top of side measure.

3. All drift boats have a bow to stern banana shape, some more than others. This shaping controls how much of the boat is in the water (subject to load factors). With the boat on a flat plane (cement floor, etc.) stand facing the bow.

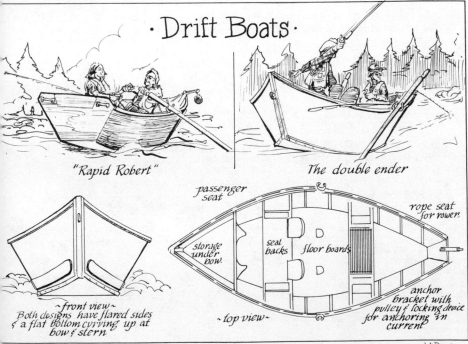

· Drift Boats ·

"Rapid Robert"

The double ender

passenger seat

storage under bow

seat backs

floor boards

rope seat for rower

anchor bracket with pulley & locking device for anchoring in current

~front view~
Both designs have flared sides & a flat bottom curving up at bow & stern

~top view~

Jeff Payne

Where does the top point of the bow hit you? If you are between 5'10" and 6' tall, the point will come somewhere between your chin and your belt buckle. The higher the better. For those boats with a lower bow and a lesser banana shaping, just figure that in rough water you may get wet, and they will usually be harder to row. Remember, too, that you mostly row a drift boat upstream and that many times you may wish to stop the boat in fast water. Ease of rowing is a definite factor for your consideration because rowing skill and ease are what keep you out of trouble.

GENERAL RULES

No one can learn drift boating from a book, but some general factors always occur and can be followed. The first requirement is an ability to handle a pair of oars. This takes coordination and practice, and no river should be attempted alone until you feel secure with oars in your hand. Here are some general rules and tips to follow:

1. Make your moves to miss obstacles well ahead of time wherever possible. Set up for what's ahead as soon as you can—don't wait until the last minute to make corrections. The rougher the water becomes, the harder the rowing becomes. *Most* of the time, if you set up well ahead, only minor corrections (or none at all) will be needed to stay in the correct path.

2. The majority of direction changes can be handled by slipping the boat from side to side while the bow remains pointed more or less downstream. Do everything you can to avoid major direction changes that call for placing the boat crossways in the current.

3. The best rule to follow when you let go of the oars is "ship them" (take them out of the water).

4. When going through really rough water don't dig the oars in deeply. If you have to row in rough water, don't dig the oars into the water deeper than the width of the blade.

5. The current will carry you safely through most tough chutes, but speed is often essential. The boat must have enough extra speed to carry you over the

Winter steelhead scene on Oregon's Wilson River. — Photo by Richard Williamson

9. Stay in the rolling waves.
Avoid the eddys and
ride it out!

8. Be cautious of
the water in which
you work your oars.

7. Hit the big waves
head on. The boat's
flat bottom creates lift.

6. Position craft
so the bow points
into the heavy
water you will hit.

5. Pull away

4.
Position the craft
so you can **pull away**
from obstacles.

3. Try to let the
current do the
work. Relax.

1. NOTE: This is only a hypothetical
set of rapids showing basic water &
boat handling techniques. Learn to
read water & when in doubt, SCOUT!

2. The point of entry should be selected
in advance with consideration of
where the current will take you.

©Jeff Dayne 1976

Drift Boat Navigation

curls (waves). If you do not have enough speed, you run the chance of sliding back down and water from the curl behind you will come over the stern.

6. Never take a rough chute or stretch of water that is new to you without beaching and looking it over. Look your rough water over from downstream looking up. This provides a good view of any rocks that may be lying too shallow 'for you to cross. Remember, too, that rivers change and bad water should never be approached lightly. Take the time to check the water ahead each time. A six-foot stump wedged between two rocks at last high water could spell disaster.

7. Don't be proud! When in doubt walk or rope (line) the boat down. Macho is stupid in a drift boat. Also, you should be prepared to put your passengers and/or equipment ashore above a bad spot. A lightened load does wonders for maneuverability.

8. Wear a flotation device. Some boaters think that the necessity for this isn't all that important on most of our Northwest rivers. Phooey! Every drift boater worth his salt will tell you that catastrophe is unpredictable. Disaster is literally a split-second occurrence. The time to don life vests is before!

9. As a novice boater the best way to learn a new river is to take a guided trip. Most guides are more than willing to give you pointers about the river as you go through. This applies also to the fishing spots. The money you spend will be really "smart money".

10. Carelessness and complacency cause more boating accidents than all other reasons combined.

The ten points listed are by no means the end-all of drift boating rules. They are listed here just to indicate *some* of the general rules you should be prepared to know and practice. Each stream is different; indeed, the same stream may differ somewhat almost daily. Of course, this is what helps make drift boating such an exciting and rewarding sport.

As to the style and design of boats, each of us hold our own opinions and preferences. For myself, I consider the Alumaweld boat designed and built by Willie Illingsworth of Medford, Oregon to be the very best around. His guide's model boat is the driest boat in rough water I've ever seen. As with all aluminum boats, something needs to be done on the bottom to counteract aluminum's high "surface tension". Aluminum boats have a tendency to stick when they run over rocks. Many boaters counteract this by covering the bottom with some material to increase the ability to slip through. My personal preference is formica. By carefully following directions any good "contact" type of cement will hold the formica to the bottom of an aluminum boat with no trouble. This material is very strong and very slick. It will allow your boat to slide over shallow rocks and, at the same time, cut down on the noise factor from the bare metal. A 4' x 12' sheet of formica will do very nicely on a 16' boat.

Inside your boat you might consider covering the floor boards with indoor/outdoor carpet. This material also helps with noise and really helps with secure footing in the boat. Once again a good contact cement will do the job.

Now, just a word about oars. Most boaters I have talked to prefer wooden oars over metal. The wood must be a hardwood. Also, if you are choosing between the seven-foot, eight-foot or nine-foot oars, go for the nine-foot. The extra length will give you much more pulling strength and better boat control.

Many boaters get into trouble because of an incorrect anchoring arrangement. If your setup for anchoring is such that you cannot cut or turn loose your anchor rope without leaving your seat, your setup is wrong. For that reason you should never knot the end of your anchor line. If something happens to cause your anchor to let go in fast, rough water—let it go—a knot at the end of the rope that would prevent free running through the pulleys could spell real trouble.

I saw this happen on the Cowlitz River, and the end result of the knot was a boat with a stern nearly pulled from the boat and two men in the water. A combination of swift water, a poorly-secured anchor rope, and a knotted line almost cost two lives and virtually destroyed a boat. This whole series of events took place in less than *ten seconds.*

OTHER BOATS

I have deliberately not disucssed other types of boats in this chapter. Jet sleds and canoes I know nothing about, having never operated either of these types. Cartop boats may be used on some rivers for steelhead, but their use is limited at best to a very few streams or to tidewater areas. Rubber rafts make me shudder. The big commercial rafts are both safe and effective in the hands of an expert and when properly equipped. The normal four- and six-man rafts you see from time to time on steelhead streams are accidents looking for a place to happen.

Taking a drift boat through some white water on an
Olympic Peninsula stream. — Photo by Trey Combs

CHAPTER SEVEN

Hints, Tips and Lies

In this chapter I will recap some of what I have said previously. Remember, no amount of reading will make you a successful drift fisherman. Drifting requires, above all, practice. It also requires patience. It took me about four years of fishing to become a consistently successful drift fisherman. I just hope that this book will help you cut that time span.

The beginner is plagued by one thing: Snags! Snags are a problem for us all, but when you first start drift fishing, you really have a problem. Several things will help you overcome the consistency of snags:

1. *Know your water.*

2. Concentrate on what you are doing during a drift—remain alert and ready to instantly pick up enough to clear a stoppage of your gear before it settles in solidly. This pick-up need not be drastic. If you are alert, you can make a very small adjustment, quickly, and your gear will clear and continue to travel.

Ninety percent of the hard snags are caused by a slow reaction, or a belly in the line. If you are snagged hard, don't fool with it—break off and start again. If you find you cannot get through a drift with enough weight to stay on bottom without snagging—move on. Chalk that drift off to conservation. If, by chance, you run into a real jerk down the line, you might tell him what a great drift it is and send him on. He'll be so busy it will keep him off the good water.

KNOW THE WATER

I suppose I have repeated this so much that by now you think, "This guy is nuts about water." Well, that's true enough—especially if it doesn't have soap in it. But, don't kid yourself, if you don't know the water you fish, you are fishing blind. After several years of drift fishing you will be able to walk into a strange area and pretty well pinpoint the good spots in a drift. Even so, you will learn about that water as you fish it. Shotgunning is a dead end in drift fishing. Pick a section of stream. Fish it over and over again until you have learned where the fish are and where they will be next trip. Remember, these fish are all looking for the same things: Rest and safety. If, under a dropping and clearing situation, a certain section of a drift provides action, this section will continue to do so under these conditions. I know many a fisherman who has a favorite area that always provides a fish or two under the right water conditions.

So, no matter how much I repeat, the fact is that the average beginner wastes time, effort and money because he is too impatient and fails to take the time to learn to read his water. Don't make this mistake!

TEMPERATURE AND LIGHT

Winter fish move through very cold water. Just as warm summer water affects the actions of the summer-run by moving them into the riffles, etc., so does the cold water of winter have its effect. The effect is one of slowing the fish down—making them logy and difficult to entice. Any time the water temperature gets down to an area below 48 degrees, the fish are less likely to respond. This is the time when patience and repetition become necessary. Where one or two drifts would pull forth a response from a fish in 50-degree water, eight or ten may be needed when the water gets down around 42 or 45 degrees. I certainly wouldn't like being in 50-degree water, but in 42-degree water I sympathize with the fish. Phooey on biting! Carrying a small thermometer with you and testing the water may help you decide how long to spend on the drift before moving on.

Sunlight also has its effect. In the summer, once the sun is on the water (except for the large rivers such as the Deschutes), fishing is over until the shadows of evening. Not so in winter. It has been my experience that the opposite is true. Time after time the fishing, under otherwise perfect conditions, hasn't become really good until the sun has hit the water—or at least until the full light of day. Many times I have hit the stream at the crack of dawn, only to have my first fish around 8:30 or 9:00 in the morning. The trouble here is that you come to the drift at 9:00 a.m., and you're last in line!

CLOTHING

A winter steelheader should expect to make his peace with nature. There's an old saying that goes: "You don't *have* to be nuts to fish steelhead, but it helps a lot." True enough, I suppose, when you consider ice, snow, rain, sleet, wind, all, perhaps, in one day. Your selection of clothing will be of major importance to you. I find that one of those "pocket warmer" heating devices is wonderful.

I personally prefer wool for my outer garments. The fact that wool gets warmer as it gets wetter is a boon on dry days that suddenly get very wet and catch you without a raincoat. Even so, a raincoat is a necessity. Just a hint: Make sure that your raincoat fits loosely enough to allow for plenty of undercoating.

BOOTS AND WADERS

Most of the time, fishing will require some wading. Either hip boots or chest waders will be called for. I suggest, if you are a beginner, that you start with hip boots. I say this for one reason only: Wading into the water, especially in winter, is dangerous. Hip boots restrict the depth you can enter and thus allow you time and practice at handling current to get used to wading. It is not a laughing matter to find yourself suddenly upended in 40-degree water. There are many types of hip boots on the market today, from ultra-light to quite heavy and stiff. I prefer a heavy type of "working" hip boot. These boots are made for work around canneries, etc., and not primarily for fishing. They have the disadvantage of being a bit heavy. The advantages, though, are many: They will stand alone, thus needn't be fastened at the belt; they are of very tough construction and are not susceptible to berry vines and barbed wire fences; they will last for years with proper care. (Hang them by the belt loops so that they don't have any standing folds or rolls.) This type of boot is not very good for summer wear, but who needs boots in the summer?

Chest waders provide for easier coverage of the water because you can wade deeper and stay dry. You can also get into trouble faster, so be careful. Carry a good stout piece of limb with you when you set off through a riffle in either boots or waders. Never go out in a pair of waders without a belt around your middle, fastened as tight as you can comfortably stand it. The belt can be used to hold your bait boxes, but its primary purpose is safety. A good tight belt will hold back water entrance into the waders for a considerable amount of time. The air trapped in the legs and feet will provide a surprising amount of flotation. These facts could be the difference between being wet but safe and being in a lot of trouble. Waders, being much more bulky than hip boots, are a drag when a great deal of water has to be covered. But when that drift just cannot be reached without wading in hip deep, and you hook a fish there every time, well . . . who worries about bulk?

Most waders and boots come with a plastic or rubber sole that is ridged in some manner to provide traction. Forget it! No traction is provided this way. Some boots or waders can be purchased with felt soles. These provide traction but are quite expensive,and the felt wears quickly. A better way is to take your boots (waders) to a shoe shop and have the soles ground smooth. Then apply a good quality (thick) piece of indoor-outdoor carpet cut to fit the foot. Several adhesives are manufactured that will hold very well. The brand I use is Plastikon 169. An industrial adhesive manufactured by B. F. Goodrich, 169 holds very well if directions are followed closely. There are other types of effective adhesives available; your local shoe repair shop should be able to advise you. Covering the soles of the boots will enable you to wade with a great deal more surefootedness and safety. I may be harping on this safety angle with boots and waders, but there is no fun involved in trying to dry out in 15-degree weather. One other point to consider: Waders and boots are worn with heavy socks, and many people tend to buy them too small. You may find the time when you will want your boots off in a hurry. If they are too small, you could be in a lot of trouble. Buy your boots or waders a size to a size and a half larger than your shoe size.

CARRYING YOUR TACKLE

Fishermen use all manner of devices to pack around their gear. I guess I have seen just about all kinds from time to time along the streams.

Nothing beats a vest! Now that's a flat statement, but it's true. A good fishing vest (buy it plenty large) will provide pocket space for your gear, ease of carrying, ease of accessibility and, most important, leave your hands free. Fishing baskets never have enough space (at least for me) and having one hanging on my side while crawling around through brush or over rocks is a nuisance. For your hardware it helps to purchase one of those small, rectangular plastic boxes. They will fit into one of the pockets easily and help to keep your spinners, etc., from getting fouled.

Craig Lasater with a bright winter-run steelhead. In 1976 Craig had the unbelievable come true. He landed a 31 pound winter-run steelhead in a Washington river.

If you like to tie your own rigs as I do, try buying a box of 2" x 3" cellophane bags for holding the ties. I purchase mine in boxes of 1,000 from Cellocraft Bag Co. in Portland. They are inexpensive to use and very convenient.

BUYING REELS AND RODS

When my wife read the section on rods and reels, she expressed derision about the advice given to take your rod with you when purchasing your reel, or vice versa. It was her contention that the store clerk would faint or protest. Perhaps she is right. The fact remains that the purchase of a good rod and reel will necessitate an expenditure quite beyond small change. Also, you must achieve as much of a balance in your equipment as you can. If you don't purchase it all at the same time or if you are adding to or replacing one or the other, test them together *before* you buy. Nothing is more disappointing or frustrating than to discover that a mistake has been made when you are a hundred miles from home and conditions are perfect for fish! Remember, price is not always indicative of quality, but it is a very good guideline!

When buying your first rod resist the temptation to go too heavy on action. Many beginners do this. I did, and I still look at that rod from time to time and wonder how I ever felt a fish with it. I have seen many, many fishermen trying to drift with a rod much more suitable to mooching for salmon from a boat than for drift fishing a small coastal stream. Actually a light, but solid, action classic will whip a fish faster than a stiff action rod. Keep the rod high and let it do the work for you. The rod must fight the fish—not the line.

SLACKING

Once in awhile a fish will get into a spot downstream from you where you cannot pressure him out. Often due to bank access it is impossible to get to him and force him back upstream. If the situation is desperate—one more run and he's into a rapid—sometimes slacking will bring him back. Back off on your line so that a belly forms below the fish. This will result in the fish feeling the pull of the line from below him rather than above, and he may move back up—away from the pull. You take a chance with this action, but there are times when the chance must be taken. It's the only avenue open to you. Also, don't let the fish get too close to you while he is still fresh. A fish that is close in and still full of fight moves too rapidly for the rod to handle his thrashing. Back away and give him room. The extra distance will give your rod recovery time and lessen the chance of the fish coming hard against slack line and snapping it.

CONSERVATION

When you have hooked a dark fish which should be released, don't remove the fish from the water if you can help it, and don't try to remove the hook if it is beyond the lip. Cut your line at the mouth and let the fish go. The hook will be destroyed by the acids in the fish's system in a very short time. The same holds true for the small migrants you often hook in the summer. The survival of the fish is worth 1,000 hooks. By the way, downstream migrants don't bite anything like summer steelhead, so don't fool with them. Pull your gear out of their way and continue your drift. Every migrant hooked and killed by a fisherman costs

All dark fish should be returned to the river. When a steelhead is dark it is a clear indication that it has just spawned or is about to.

you money. The planting program of your game department is far from inexpensive. These agencies need help and encouragement—not some fool coming in behind and catching a "nice mess of trout."

Conservation is not an idea—it's a way of life. To me, any fisherman who is not also a conservationist is a fool. When you consider the gill nets, dams, logging, mining, irrigation, garbage, pollution, you name it, affecting our streams and the fish—you must fight for conservation or you lose. Unless the sports fishermen wise up and begin to organize and fight there is little hope. The Northwest Steelheaders is one sportsmen's conservation organization I strongly recommend to you. Having merged with Trout Unlimited (a national conservaton organization), they have become the Northwest Steelheaders Council of Trout Unlimited, taking in Washington, Oregon and Idaho. How many times have I heard fishermen gripe about the state of the fishing and the decline of the runs. Put your money where your mouth is, brother: Join up!

Consider this one factor out of all of the rest: How can we justify a freshwater commercial harvest of an anadromous fish run in 1976 using methods dating back to 1800? Any way you look at the problem, biologically, economically, or in terms of efficient management, the procedure is not only unsound—it is insane. It continues, and will continue, until the sportsmen wise up and join up!

While I am speaking about the Steelheaders, let me invite you to one of our Steelhead Clinics. Various chapters of our organization conduct these clinics, usually in the fall, giving displays and talks on tackle, methods, techniques, water reading, etc. These clinics are either free or the charge is minimal, prizes are given, and a good time is had by all. Check your local sports shop or newspaper fishing editor for dates and times. Better still—join the Steelheaders chapter nearest you.

PICK A RIVER

Many fishermen ask me at the clinics: Where do I go to catch fish? My answer always is: Pick a river! Now, friends, a large part of the fun of drift fishing is the thrill of discovery. Far be it from me to take that thrill away from you. However, your state agency or commission charged with sport fishing management will have, for the asking, information on where to go, catch ratios, peak run periods, etc. A little research will head you in the right direction. Ask another fisherman where he was fishing when he caught the twenty-pounder, and, if he's smart, he'll say: "On the bank," or "in the water."

My partner and I were fishing one day on a small coast stream for fall salmon. The drift we were fishing was a small one, suitable for one, and we were stretching it to fish two. We had been there an hour when along came two more guys complete with tackle boxes and a huge gaff hook. It became immediately obvious that they planned to step in and let fly. Well, friends, that's not "fishing" to this writer, and if the day comes when I have to crowd into water like that in order to fish, I quit. One of these "fishermen" made the remark that four wasn't too many—last week there were ten. When I saw his gear I knew what kind of "fishing" was going on. The only puzzle was why he bothered with a rod at all: Why not just start with the gaff? If I could only fish on another man's drift and then use gear calculated to snag, I'm afraid my fishing would consist of a trip to the market—cheaper, faster and every bit as much sport.

It is my hope that somewhere in this book you may have found something that will help you in your quest for these fish. If by chance we meet on the bank of a stream, let's agree on one rule: How to—any time; where to—never!

GOOD FISHING

CHAPTER EIGHT

Caring For, Preserving and Cooking Your Fish

The quality of the steelhead trout as food is, and will probably continue to be, subject to continual debate. To those who enjoy fish as food however, the winter runs of these rainbow trout do have a place and are very tasty given proper preparation. I shall make no attempt to rank the anadromous salmonids here—each of you will have your own preference. Just remember that the real key to flavor will be how the fish is handled. Some general rules are:

1. Clean the fish as soon as possible after they have been caught. Don't let the fish flop around any more than necessary. Fish are of delicate flesh and bruise easily. Remove the entrails and gills right away and scrape out the blood line along the back. Hanging the fish by the tail will improve bleeding.

2. Whenever possible keep a fish cool. Don't, however, return a cleaned fish to the water—water will work to soften the flesh.

3. In hot weather where ice is not available to you, air is your best friend. Dry the fish inside and out as thoroughly as possible (dry grass is a good thing to use for this) and hang out of the direct sun. Prop the belly cavity open with a stick. The fish will stiffen and glaze as it dries; this glaze will prevent fly damage. Fish may be kept quite easily up to 24 hours this way by keeping them dry, well-aired and out of the direct sunlight. A short dip in cold water will restore the fish quickly to its former freshness.

4. As soon as possible get fish to be transported into ice. Keep them out of the ice water, however.

5. Always re-clean your fish when you get home prior to preserving. Remove the head, tail and fins as well as any remaining bits of blood, etc. in the belly cavity.

6. It is not necessary to scale trout and salmon, but the slime on the skin should be removed. Wash the fish in a solution of one part vinegar to three parts water and rinse with clean water.

PRESERVING YOUR FISH

Canning and freezing are the two most popular methods of preserving fish, but they are by no means the only methods available. Steelhead trout or salmon may be pickled, corned, smoked, dried, dry salted, etc. These methods are often easier and cheaper than canning and freezing. Home preserving by methods other than canning or freezing will be discussed separately for each method, but some general points should be considered. The home-cured product has one big enemy: Bacteria. Bacteria feed in a warm, moist environment. The rule of thumb is: No air, no light, store at less than 70°.

CANNING

Salmon:

Remove scales, fins, and head. Clean and wash thoroughly. Leave backbone. Cut into can-length pieces. Soak in brine (one cup salt to one gallon water) for one hour. This will do for 25 pounds of salmon. Drain for several minutes and fill container. Pack solidly but do not crush.

In Glass Jars—Seal and process.

In C-enamel Tin Cans—Crimp lid loosely and steam fifteen minutes. Complete seal and process immediately.

	Time to Process
Pint jars	100 minutes at 10 pounds
No. 2 tins	100 minutes at 10 pounds

Smoked Salmon:

Smoking followed by canning is a favorite method of preserving salmon. Fillet salmon, soak in a brine solution.

Most people do not like too strong a smoke flavor, and, since canning intensifies the smoke flavor, salmon fillets for canning should be cold-smoked only two to three hours or until light brown.

The fillets are then cut in can lengths, packed in the can, sealed, and processed the same as fresh salmon. It is recommended that smoked salmon be canned in C-enamel (seafood formula) cans. The cans and jars should be cooled well in air before storing.

	Time to Process
½ Pint jars	95 minutes at 10 pounds
½ lb. C-enamel flat tins	90 minutes at 10 pounds
No. 2 C-enamel tins	100 minutes at 10 pounds

If a stronger smoke flavor is desired, salmon can be hot-smoked or kippered until a golden brown. When hot smoking in your own portable smoker, smoke the fish for from four to five hours, then can as above.

FREEZING

Although many people freeze by other methods, my favorite is freezing in water. Frankly, if you intend to keep your fish longer than three months, you should always freeze in water. Using quart, half-gallon or gallon milk cartons is the most inexpensive way. Simply add water to cover the amount of steaks or fillets in your container. Frozen water does evaporate, so you should check your containers from time to time to be sure that no part of the fish extends above the ice.

The secret to fish frozen in an ice block is in the thawing. Do not let the thawing fish stay in the thawing water, and thaw fast. The best way I have found is to tear off the container, place the block of ice and fish in a colander and run cold water over the ice to speed thawing. The colander allows the water to drain away. As soon as the fish is free from the ice, remove it from the colander and set it aside to finish thawing.

U.S. Department of Agriculture Home and Garden Bulletin No. 93, "Freezing Meat and Fish in the Home," pages 14-17, has excellent illustrations and information on cleaning, dressing and wrapping fish for the home freezer. Ask for a free copy from your nearest Extension office.

Whole or Cut?

Decide how you want to serve the fish. Leave them whole for baking or boiling, or cut in chunks, steaks or fillets, depending on the way you want to cook and serve them.

Package:

All your work is wasted if packaging is poor. Use only good quality, new, freezer packaging material. Heavy aluminum foil is good; so is laminated frozen meat wrapping paper. Polyethylene sheets and bags are moisture-vapor proof, too, and when covered with stockingette for added protection the package is easy to handle. Freezing jars and tins can be purchased. These are best for freezing but take the most room in the freezer and cost the most.

Add some moisture in the package. Wrap loosely in vegetable parchment paper dipped in cold water before wrapping in the moisture-vapor-proof paper, or dip fish for thirty seconds in a salt solution (2/3 cup salt in one gallon of water), before putting it in the freezer wrapping material. Commercial fisheries glaze fish before storage. They dip the frozen fish in ice water and freeze it again. A second dip follows to thicken the glaze. The fish is then wrapped or packaged in moisture-vapor-proof material. Do not tear, puncture, or scuff the package after it is wrapped. Handle each package carefully before and after freezing. If air gets to the fish, the oxygen quickly causes rancidity.

Freeze:

Spread packages to freeze. Turn control to coldest position (0° or lower) so the fish will freeze quickly.

Store:

Frozen fish should be zero (0° F.) or colder. How long fish will keep depends on the kind of fish. Lean fish keeps longer than does fat fish. If handled well and packaged properly, fish may keep up to nine months. Usually three to six months is proper storage life of fish. Fish in vacuum glass or tin containers will keep longer. If only fresh fish are frozen and they are adequately protected, there will be no odors of fish in the freezer. Absorption of fish odor by butter or other foods in the freezer means that the packaging material is not keeping the air out or that stale fish were frozen.

Refreeze?

Fish is such a perishable food that refreezing breaks the cells and causes a loss of texture, and if thawed completely before refreezing, the flavor will be affected.

SMOKING AND SMOKEHOUSES

The following are some general facts about smoking fish, including some simple directions for building your own smoker.

FIG 1. Smoked fish can be produced at home with simple equipment: An old wood range, a length of stove pipe with 2 elbows and a barrel

Fish are smoked as a means of preserving the meat, but also for the pleasant taste contributed by the smoke. Smoked fish is cooked fish and subject to spoilage even under the most sanitary conditions. Refrigeration must be used to extend the storage life of most smoked fish. Canned or frozen smoked fish is a great delicacy and can be produced at home with simple equipment.

Smoking Salmon for Canning:

Dress fish as usual. Split dressed fish on either side of backbone, removing the backbone. Remove gills but leave the bony plates to support the weight when hanging in the smokehouse. Rinse with fresh water to remove blood, slime, and waste material. Score the fish, cutting several slits in the skin to improve salt penetration.

Make a saturated brine solution by adding six cups salt to one gallon of clean water (it will float a potato). Use a clean plastic container or crock.

Immerse the fish in the brine and let stand for 30 minutes to 1½ hours, depending on size of the fish or thickness of the pieces. The sides from a 15 to 20 pound fish must be brined approximately one hour.

Remove from brine and rinse lightly with fresh, cold water, just enough to remove salt from surface. Drain well. Blot surface with clean paper towels and let dry until surface is dry and shiny. Moving air will do this in 15 or 20 minutes.

If you wish a dry salt or mild cure fish for smoking, the fish must be freshened by placing in cold running water overnight, or for approximately fifteen hours after brining. Drain and dry as above.

There are two methods of smoking salmon—by cold smoke or by hot smoke. A light cold smoked flavor is best for canning because the canning process intensifies it. Any non-resinous wood, such as alder, may be used for smoking.

Cold Smoked Salmon:

Smoke four to seven hours, depending on the size of the fish, in cool dense smoke (not over 100° F.) or until the surface is light brown.

Hot Smoked Salmon (Kippered):

Smoke three to five hours, depending on the size of the fish, gradually raising the temperature of the smokehouse from 160° to 190° F., or until fish are cooked and have a light brown surface color.

If you wish to can smoked fish, the next step is to cut into can-height pieces.

Pack as for plain salmon, omitting salt. One-half pound flat cans are preferred. If desired, add one tablespoon of vegetable oil per can.

Follow directions for use of pressure cooker. Exhaust same as for plain salmon. Process one-half pound flat cans for 90 minutes at 240° F. (10 pounds pressure).

Making a Smokehouse:

A simple plywood smokehouse was designed and constructed by personnel of the Pascagoula Technological Laboratory of the U.S. Bureau of Commercial Fisheries. The 4' x 4' x 4' smoker was built by unskilled labor in sixteen hours. The firebox is a 55-gallon drum with removable clamp-on lid and a door cut out near the bottom for feeding wood. A stovepipe runs from the drum to the smokehouse, and a baffle is placed over the stovepipe opening to disperse the smoke inside the house. Exhaust holes in the sides, back and front near the top allow the smoke to escape. Wood sealer is applied to the outside to prevent warping, and removable trays slide on wood runners.

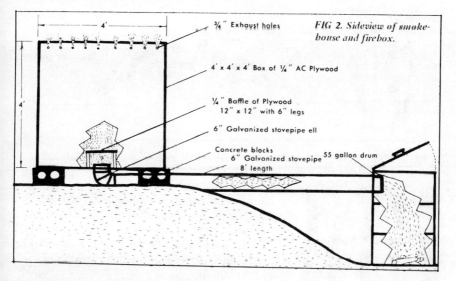

¾" Exhaust holes

FIG 2. *Sideview of smokehouse and firebox.*

4' x 4' x 4' Box of ¼" AC Plywood

¼" Baffle of Plywood 12" x 12" with 6" legs

6" Galvanized stovepipe ell

Concrete blocks
6" Galvanized stovepipe 8' length

55 gallon drum

Methods of Hanging Fish for Smoking:

Small fish may be hung on one or more S-shaped hooks (Fig. 2B) or, if split, on two rods run through flesh beneath the bony neckplates (Fig. 2A). Figures 2C and 2D are other ways of hanging filleted or split fish for smoking.

Smoking Method for Sportsmen:

Sport fishermen may wish to preserve part of their catch immediately by using this simple smoking method. It is especially good for trout, pike, or pickeral, but may be used successfully with almost any medium-sized fish.

Cut off heads and gut fish. Cut above the backbone almost to the tail; make another cut below the backbone and break off, leaving about 1/5 of the tail section uncut to the fish lies flat in one piece. Score the fish lengthwise from head to tail, cutting ¼" deep slashes about 1" apart. Wash fish thoroughly. Wipe dry and rub inside and out with a mixture of one ounce pepper to one pound salt.

Store fish overnight in a cool place. Next morning rinse thoroughly. Spread the fish open using several thin, flat sticks pointed at the ends to pierce the skin.

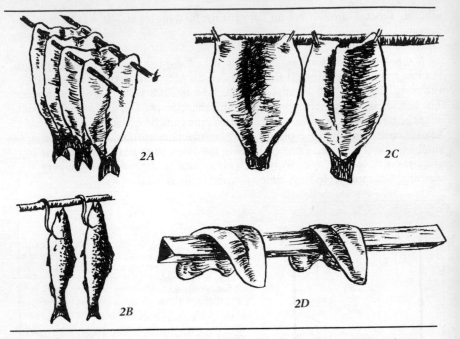

2A

2C

2B

2D

Use two or three across the back of the fish. Hang in the breeze about three hours until fish dries and a thin surface skin forms

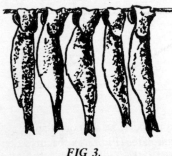

FIG 3.

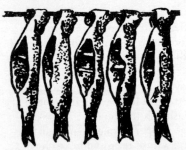

Store fish overnight in a cool place. Next morning rinse thoroughly. Spread fish open using several thin, flat sticks pointed at the ends to pierce the skin. Use two or three across the back of the fish. Hang in the breeze about three hours until fish dries and a thin surface skin forms (Fig. 3).

While the fish dries, dig a shallow pit about three feet wide and prepare a bed of red coals. Hardwood fuel such as birch, aspen, or alder may be used. Fasten each fish to the forked end of a stick four to five feet long. Thrust the other end into the ground so it hangs over the coals at an angle. Place sticks far enough apart so fish do not touch.

A second method is to fasten two or three fish across a stick so they do not touch, then thrust the stick into the ground, but not as close to the fire as in the other method.

Make a tripod of poles above the smoke-sticks and cover with a thick layer of green boughs and grass. Leave a hole near the ground. Place green wood on the coals to build up dense smoke and cover the hole. From time to time add fresh green wood to the fire. Smoke fish six to eighteen hours, depending on size and degree of smoking desired. Cool fish, wrap and store in a dry, cool place. The smoked fish will keep in good condition two to four weeks.

Luch's Own Recipe for Smoked Steelhead or Salmon:

In addition to the general information above, here is my own recipe for smoked steelhead or salmon. I say my own because it is the one I use, not because I invented it. I don't know the true background of the recipe; I just know it makes the best smoked fish, turkey, chicken, etc. I have ever eaten.

Before discussing the recipe, just a few words about portable commercial smokers. When you purchase this type of smoker, you should remember that the temperature control on the heat unit is not uniform in operation between smokers. This fact means that each smoker will have its own time factor due to differences in heat. These time differentials will usually result in a thirty-minute to one-hour differential in smoking time. Only experience with your particular smoker will tell you, but smoking time for fish will usually be between seven and nine hours. The size and thickness of the pieces of fish will also influence this timing. Smoking is a two-step operation: Brining and smoking. Brining the fish will take about six hours for fresh fish with this recipe. If you freeze the fish first, you can cut this time considerably. If you plan to smoke a fish, freeze it whole and unwrapped for three to five days prior to smoking, then thaw, cut up and brine. The freezing removes moisture from the flesh and, when the fish is brined, increases the speed of absorption of the brine.

The Brine

2 cups Plain Salt	½ tsp. Season Salt (Johnny's, Lowrey's,
1 pound Dark Brown Sugar	etc.)
½ tsp. Garlic Powder	4 tbsp. Molasses
½ tsp. Wright's Liquid Smoke	½ gal. Water

Dissolve ingredients in water. Cut fish into smoking-sized chunks (leave skin on and backbone in). Soak in large bowl or bucket (plastic) six hours for fresh fish or 1½ hours for frozen fish. Remove from brine and pat pieces dry. Pepper fish if desired (try lemon pepper). Let stand until shiny glaze forms. Place on racks and smoke. The portable type of hot smoker will take seven to nine hours in most cases.

Now a word about smoking woods. In the portable type of smoker you will use either chips or sawdust, allowing this material to smolder, thus making smoke. Any non-resinous hardwood will do for smoking, and packages of this wood can be purchased at many sporting goods stores. Some of the woods that impart good flavor for smoking are: Alder, vine maple, hickory, ash, cherry, apple, plum, etc.

Also, you should remember that fish will only absorb so much smoke. Usually this absorption takes place during the first four hours of smoking. With the portable smokers you only need fill your pan with wood three times (this will take care of your first four hours of smoking). From here on heat will finish the job, and you will largely waste any added wood.

Norwegian Smoked Pressed Salmon:

After cleaning as usual, cut off tail and head. Then cut along spine and remove backbone. Spread flat and hold down edges of back skin with wooden picks. Cover with salt and sugar—one quart salt to one cup sugar. Press between two wide boards with a small weight on the top board for two to three days, depending on the size of the salmon.

Remove the salt mixture with a cloth. Wash fish with one teaspoon saltpeter dissolved in ¼ cup of brandy or water. Smoke for eight hours in cool alder smoke. Let salmon hang for about six days before use.

The backbone, head, and tail can be cooked and the meat removed and used separately.

DRY SALTING AND BRINE SALTING

Temporary preservation or corning while fishing:

Sportsmen fishing a considerable distance from home frequently bring home fish in poor condition and throw them away. Such waste can be avoided if a few precautions are taken. Carry with you a mixture of salt and pepper (one tablespoon pepper to one cup salt).

Clean fish as usual and rub cavity well with the salt and pepper mixture. Rub some into the skin, too.

Place the fish in a basket or box with a loose packing of green leaves around the fish. Cover the container with several thicknesses of burlap. Leave an air space between the burlap and the fish. Moisten it and keep it moistened as evaporation lowers the temperature in the container.

Treated in this way, the fish should remain in good condition for at least 24 hours, or until ice is available. When rinsed thoroughly the fish is treated in any way desired—cooked immediately, canned or frozen, or brined and smoked. Should it be necessary to keep the fish for several days, roll in salt and pack away in a container with as much salt as will cling to them, and they will keep for about ten days. Treated with this heavy salting, the fish will have to be freshened for about twelve hours in two or three changes of fresh water.

Brine Salting:

The family salting fifty pounds or less of salt fish needs no special equipment except a sharp knife and a two to four-gallon container. This may be a stone crock, a wooden barrel, or a tub or a plastic container such as a new plastic garbage can with a lid.

Salt should be as pure and as clean as can be purchased. It should be free from carbonates or magnesium. Dairy salt is good.

Lean fish are salted more easily than oily fish. The salt brine penetrates it better, and it doesn't become rancid so easily. However, if oily fish are well salted, they are of the finest quality. Both saltwater and freshwater fish can be brine salted.

The method of brining is the same for all varieties. Smaller fish are split down the back so as to lie flat. Large fish are split into two fillets, removing the backbone. The gills are always removed, but the collarbone just below is not cut away. The collarbone is needed to support the weight of the piece when handled, especially if the brined fish is to be smoked. Without this, the piece will drop from the smokehouse hangers during the smoking.

For good penetration of salt, the flesh of the thickest pieces may be scored lengthways to a depth of half an inch and from one to two inches apart. Cut carefully so as not to penetrate the skin. The pieces should be cut only large enough to lie flat on the bottom of the crock or container.

After the fish is cleaned and soaked in brine to draw off diffused blood, the pieces are left to drain while you get the salt ready. Use a large dish pan or make a shallow box about two feet square with sides six inches high and fill with dry salt. Scatter a thin layer of salt on the bottom of the crock or container. Dredge each piece of fish with salt and rub some salt into the scored places in the heavier pieces. Pack with the skin side down and arrange so the pieces make an even layer. See the illustration in Figure 4. Scatter a thin layer of salt over each layer of fish and repeat the dredging of fish and arrange the next layer at right angles to the one below.

FIG. 4

FIG. 5

With large fish the pieces with the backbone are placed next to the wall of the container. An extra piece may be placed in the middle, to level the layer, if needed. The pieces should overlap each other as little as possible. Small fish are packed in a ring with the tip of the head touching the walls of the container. It may be necessary to lay one or two fish across the center to keep the layer level. Stagger successive layers so that each fish rests on two fish of the layer below. Scatter salt between each layer. *The top layer* of fish, both large and small, *should be packed skin side up* (Fig. 5).

The amount of salt to be used depends on the season of the year, the size and fatness of the fish, and the probably length of preservation. A general rule is to use one part of salt to three parts fish. Add a little for especially fat fish and for preserving for a long period of time without refrigeration, smoking or in hot weather. Remember that an excess of salt will "burn" the fish and lower the quality.

Place a loosely-fitting wooden cover or china plate on the top layer of fish and weight the cover down with fair-sized rocks or bricks—well-washed for this purpose. The fish will form its own brine. Small fish will be completely brined in 48 hours. Thicker and fatter fish will require a week or eight days.

At the end of this time, the fish are removed, scrubbed in fresh saturated brine (six cups of salt to one gallon of water) with a stiff brush and then smoked or repacked with a very light scattering of salt between the layers. Fill the crock

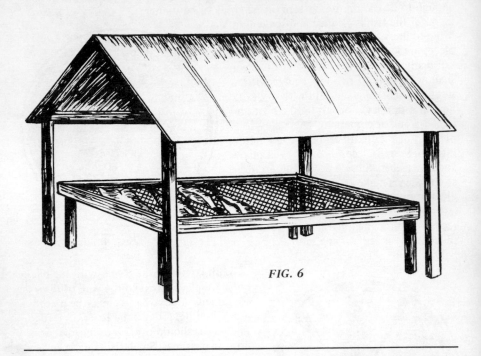

FIG. 6

or container with a fresh saturated salt brine and store in a cool, dark place. After three months, or at the first sign of fermentation, change the brine again. *Do not keep longer than nine months!*

Dry Salting:

Properly dry-salted fish will keep longer than brine-salted fish. The fish are prepared as described for brine-salting and filleted and scored if large. Small fish should be split down the back. The fish are cleaned and drained before dredging with salt.

After salting, stack the fish in rows on a rack, choosing a place where the brine formed will run away. First, scatter a thin layer of salt on the place where the fish are to be stacked. Alternate the fish heads and tails and scatter a little salt between the layers. Fish are piled flesh side up, except for the last layer, which is laid skin side up. The average amount of salt used is one part salt to four parts fish.

The fish are taken out of salt after 48 hours or in one week, depending upon the size and the weather. In damp or stormy weather they are allowed to remain in salt longer. Less time is required for salting in warm weather.

When the fish are ready for drying, they should be scrubbed in brine to remove all excess salt. No traces of salt should be visible. Drain for fifteen or twenty minutes before arranging on the drying racks.

Drying racks are roofed over frames of wood covered with chicken wire and standing on legs about four feet high. A slat top of thin poles or laths two inches apart may be substituted for the wire mesh. See Figure 6.

FIG. 7

Fish should be kept shaded at all times during drying. A breezy location should be chosen if possible. If only a few fish are being dried, they may be hung under a wide overhanging eave, or from the rafters of a shed or barn where there is good cross ventilation (Fig. 7).

If placed on racks, the fish are laid skin side down but should be turned three or four times the first day. The fish are gathered up and stored each night to prevent molding and decay where dew is heavy. The fish are stacked heads and tails on floor racks as before and covered with a weight at least as heavy as the fish, to press out further moisture. No stack should be more than two feet high. If at any time the weather is unfavorable and the fish cannot be put out to dry, repile each day with the top fish at the bottom and the bottom fish at the top of the pile. If several days are bad for drying, added salt may be needed.

A smoke or smudge under the drying racks may be necessary, for the first day at least, to keep the flies away. The smudge should always be of "green" deciduous leaves and branches to make a heavy smudge. Evergreens give off a resinous smoke.

The usual test for dryness is to press the thick part of the flesh with the thumb and forefinger. If no impression can be made, the fish are sufficiently dried. The cured fish are wrapped in waxed paper, packed in a thin wooden box, tightly covered, and stored away in a cool, dry place. At the first sign of rust, mold or reddening, scrub the fish off in a salt brine and dry in the air for a day or two.

SPICED FISH

Here are two recipes for spiced fish, one for canning and one for immediate use:

Spiced Fish:

Salmon, shad, mackerel, trout, or lake trout may be used. Scrape off all scales, remove fins and heads, clean, and wash fish thoroughly, but do not take out backbones. Cut cleaned fish into can-length pieces and soak these in brine, in the proportion of one-half pound of salt to one gallon of water for one hour. Drain fish for about ten minutes.

Vinegar Sauce

2 quarts Vinegar	¼ ounce Whole Cloves
1 quart Water	1/8 ounce Cracked Cardamom Seed
2 ounces (¼ cup) Sugar	1/8 ounce Bay Leaves
¼ ounce Whole White Pepper	1/8 ounce Cracked Whole Ginger
¼ ounce Mustard Seed	

Add sugar and water to vinegar. Tie spices loosely in cheesecloth and simmer in vinegar solution for one hour. Strain.

Fill containers, but pack rather loosely and add one-half strength vinegar sauce. Exhaust in both tin cans and glass jars by cooking in open can or jar for twenty minutes.

Invert the containers on a wire screen and drain for about three minutes. Right the containers and add a slice or two of raw onion, a bay leaf, a few mixed spices, and enough fresh vinegar sauce, full strength, to cover fish. One tablespoon olive oil may be added if desired.

In glass jars—pack and process. In plain tin cans—pack, clinch loosely, exhaust for ten minutes, seal, and process.

Time to Process

½ Pint Jars	90 minutes at 10 pounds
½ Pound Plain Tin	80 minutes at 10 pounds

Spiced Fish No. 2:

Mix heavy solution of salt water in large pot (three quarts of salt water). Heat to dissolve salt. Add four cloves chopped garlic, one small chopped onion, one stick chopped celery, one-half cup pickling spice, one-eighth cup white vinegar. Bring to a boil and simmer for 1½ to two hours. Reboil and add chunks (about 2" square) of filleted, skinned salmon or steelhead. Boil for two or three minutes. Simmer for ½ to ¾ hour. Last fifteen minutes add one cup red wine. Serve hot or cold. If served hot, try topping with dressing made by mixing mayonnaise and catsup until pink, add dash of Worcestershire sauce and dash of tabasco.

PICKLED FISH

Many different fish lend themselves to pickling: fall and coho salmon (freshwater-caught are best because of lessened oil in flesh), steelhead trout, shad (males only—females have softer flesh), herring, smelt, etc.

Pickled Herring, Shad, Salmon or Steelhead (serves 6-8):

Prepare fish by filleting, cutting into one-inch cubes, and placing in crock or plastic bucket in layers. Place generous layer of rock salt between each layer of fish. If left in salt brine more than twelve hours fish must be soaked out in cold water overnight before pickling. If twelve hours or less, simply wash and pat dry.

Pickling Brine

¾ cup White Vinegar
½ cup Water
½ cup Sugar
2-3 pounds cubed fish (use only male shad; coho pickle best of all salmon species)
1½" piece Fresh Horseradish Root, scraped and thinly sliced, or substitute 2 tbsp. Prepared Horseradish drained and squeezed dry in a kitchen towel

1 medium Carrot, peeled and thinly sliced (¾ cup)
2 small Onions, peeled and thinly sliced (preferably red)
¼" piece Ginger Root, thinly sliced (optional; try it with or without to suit your taste)
2 tsp. Allspice
2 tsp. Whole Yellow Mustard Seeds
2 large or 3 small Bay Leaves

Bring vinegar, sugar and water to a boil in an enameled or stainless steel saucepan. Stir to dissolve sugar. Cool liquid to room temperature. Use a quart or half-gallon mason jar and arrange remaining ingredients in layers—onions, fish, carrots, spices—layer on layer until ingredients are used up. Pour cooled pickling liquid into jar; it must just cover the contents. (Make more liquid if needed.) Close jar securely (tightly) and refrigerate four four days to one week. Serve as an appetizer right from the jar or place in a shallow bowl and mix with sour cream to coat fish and onions, etc. for a different flavor effect. Will keep in refrigerator for up to 45 days.

Spiced Herring:

Prepare 25 pounds of herring. Clean, remove backbone and fins and wash well. Pack in a crock and cover with vinegar and let stand for 24 hours.

Salt and Spice Mixture

1¼ pounds Salt	½ ounce White Pepper
¾ pound Sugar	1 ounce Long-Pod Peppers
1 ounce Cinnamon	1 ounce Chili Pepper
½ ounce Allspice	½ ounce Hops, or 30 drops Oil of Hops
½ ounce Cloves	1 qt. Onion, sliced thinly

Remove fish from the vinegar and let it drain. Place a layer of herring in the scalded crock and sprinkle with the salt and spice mixture, adding a few slices of onion. Continue layering until all fish are used. Weight the fish with a clean plate or board with a weight on top to keep all the fish under the brine that will develop. The fish is ready for use after four or five weeks and will keep in a cool place all winter. Serve as it comes from the crock without washing it.

Pickled Herring—Norwegian Style:

Clean eight medium herring and cover with one quart brine (one-quarter cup salt to one quart water) for thirty minutes. Remove from the brine and wipe dry. Place in a crock with alternate layers of fish and the following mixture:

1 Onion, sliced	a few Whole Cloves
¼ Lemon, sliced	2 Bay Leaves
1 tsp. Whole Peppers	¼ tsp. Allspice

Cover with one-half quart vinegar and one-half quart water solution. Place the crock in a kettle of cold water and bring it to a boil. The herring is ready to use when the meat drops from the bones. Chill and serve cold.

Pickled Salmon:

Simmer or steam in salted water (one tablespoon salt to one quart water) a four-pound chunk of salmon in a cheesecloth for 45 minutes. Drain, and keep one cup of the cooking water and add two cups of vinegar, one ounce whole pepper, 1½ ounces nutmeg (grated fresh is best), and one ounce mace. Cook five minutes and cool. When cold, pour over the cold salmon and add two tablespoons of salad oil. Cover, and store in a cool, dry place. The pickled salmon will keep for several months.

Spiced Salted Herring:

Clean five salted herring and soak for two to three hours in equal parts of milk and water and drain. Remove backbones, heads and fins and cut in convenient size pieces (half to one-inch slices) and place in jars with alternate thin slices of onions. Mix and bring only to a boil:

1 cup Vinegar	¼ cup Sugar
1/3 cup Salad Oil	3 Bay Leaves
1/3 cup Water	½ tsp. Whole Pepper

When cool, pour over the herring in the jars, and seal. The herring are ready to serve after 24 hours and will keep for several weeks.

Herring Anchovies:

Clean herring, remove backbone, head and fins. Cut in two-inch lengths, enough to make two quarts of herring. Soak in a heavy brine (one cup salt to two cups water). Mix well:

2 tbsp. Salt	1 tsp. Hops
1 tsp. Cloves	2 tbsp. Sugar
2 tbsp. Pepper	a few Bay Leaves

Alternate drained fish and salt mixture in a crock or canning jar. Seal. It is ready to use after three weeks.

Canned Fish Balls:

1 medium Salmon or other Saltwater	1 tsp. White Pepper (or more to taste)
Fish (about ten pounds)	1 tsp. Mace
1 button Garlic	3 Eggs
1 small Onion	3 cups Water (or more to make a paste)
1 tbsp. Salt (or more to taste)	

Fillet the fish. Put fish bones and head in a kettle with enough water to cover them. Cook slowly while you prepare the fish balls. Put the fillets, onions and garlic through a food chopper, twice. Use the fine blade. Add the salt and seasonings and stir or mix well with a wooden spoon or the hands. Add one egg and one cup water at a time and work into a smooth paste. Repeat, adding one egg and one cup water until the three eggs and three cups water are used. Add more water if needed. Shape into balls.

Strain the bones from the fish stock. Bring it to a boil. Drop the fish balls into the boiling stock a few at a time and cook for ten minutes. Pack fish balls in tins or cans to within ¾" of the top. Fill with the boiling stock. Seal and process in the pressure canner for 60 minutes at 10 pounds of pressure.

To serve, make an egg sauce of the broth and serve over the heated fish balls.

CHOWDER

One of the most interesting dishes than can be concocted using salmon or steelhead trout is a chowder. Most people throw away the parts of a fish that are best for a good chowder and thereby waste some delicious eating. The tips, cheeks, backbone and head trimmings provide the richest and most flavorful portions of the fish. By trimming and saving these sections (freeze in water until sections from two or three fish are collected), a marvelously hearty chowder can be prepared, either for instant use or for canning.

The cheeks of a salmon or steelhead lie just behind the eye and are somewhat cone-shaped. The meat is pale, solid and very flavorful.

The heavy fins just behind the head (pectoral) and those at the vent (ventral) provide the tips. The backbone (removed by filleting) can be cut into sections, and the head can be trimmed at the top rear all the way forward until cartilage is reached. All of this meat is heavy in fats and oils and is highly flavored. After cooking in the chowder, the bony parts may be removed with a slotted spoon, leaving just the meat, which will fall away.

Essentially you use a standard recipe for clam chowder (New England type), substituting salmon, etc. for clams. The following is a concentrated recipe for canning, but the cook may make simple changes for an immediate meal. Probably the best fish to use here is the spring chinook. Next best would be summer steelhead or ocean-caught coho and fall chinook.

New England Clam or Fish Chowder:

Flesh from backbones, heads or other portions of fish may be utilized. The amounts in the formula given here are sufficient for one dozen No. 2 cans or pint jars.

5 lbs. diced Potato	2 qts. Fish Broth*
9 cups Clams or 5 lbs. Boned Fish	2 tbsp. Salt
(edible portion)	½ tsp. Pepper
¾ lb. Salt Pork (fat back)	½ cup Flour
¾ lb. chopped Onion	

*Fish broth is obtained by cooking edible scraps of fish in water in the proportion of about four pounds of scraps to one gallon of water. Backbones and heads or other portions of fish may be utilized. The mixture is allowed to simmer for two hours, after which it is strained and the scraps discarded.

Grind the pork and onions, then cook them together in a preserving kettle until they are soft, but not brown.

Beat the flour slowly into the fish broth until a smooth, milky liquid is obtained. Add this to the kettle together with the salt and pepper, and simmer contents to a boiling point.

Fill ¾ cup of diced potato and ¾ cup of fish into each No. 2 can or pint jar. To prevent discoloration, potatoes should be blanched immediately after dicing or kept in water until needed. Some canners find it better to steam the fish in a pressure cooker and then flake it than to use raw fish.

After adding the fish and potatoes, fill each container with hot fish broth and seal immediately.

This is a concentrated chowder. Dilute with an equal quantity of milk when heating for serving.

Time to Process

Pint jars	90 minutes at 10 pounds
No. 2 tins	80 minutes at 10 pounds

POACHING

Salmon, steelhead trout, trout and many other varieties of fish lend themselves to preparation by poaching. The method is quite simple, but the results can be outstanding. Use a good skillet or frying pan with fairly straight sides, medium heat, steaks or fillets of fish, and any of a large variety of poaching liquids. Some of the general rules to follow are: Don't boil, don't salt before cooking (salt will kill the flavor of some of the liquids used), don't be afraid to experiment with different liquids.

The liquid should come approximately halfway up the sides of the pieces of fish, and you should spoon the liquid over the fish as it cooks. Cooking time is short and should be terminated when the flesh becomes flaky. Some of the liquids to try are: Milk (also buttermilk), beer (both flat and fresh), wine (a good white such as a California sauterne or a crisp chablis), tomato juice (try V-8 or Snappy Tom).

By holding the liquid just under a boil, cooking time will usually be less than fifteen minutes.

By the way, fish cooks well with wine in almost all recipes, but there is a good rule to follow: If you can't drink the wine, don't cook with it. Those wines labeled "cooking type" almost always have salt added. Phooey! Most fish cooks best when the salt is added at the table, and that is always true when using wine. Try drinking wine with salt added, and you will see what I mean.

Poached Salmon or Steelhead:

2 tbsp. Butter (softened)	1 small Bay Leaf
2 tbsp. Onions, finely chopped	1 tsp. Salt
2 tbsp. Fresh Parsley, finely chopped	Fresh-Ground Black Pepper
4-6 Fillets about 1" thick	1½ cups Hard Cider or Dry White Wine
8 Fresh Musroom Caps, sliced	1 Egg Yolk
3 Tomatoes, peeled, seeded and cut	1/3 cup Heavy Cream
into 2" x ¼" strips	1 tsp. Lemon Juice

Preheat oven to 375°. Butter sides and bottom of shallow baking dish. Spread with chopped onions and parsley and lay fish on top. Scatter broken bay leaf, mushrooms and tomato strips on top and season with salt and a few grindings of pepper. Pour cider or wind down side of dish and bring to simmer over moderate heat. Cover with piece of buttered waxed paper and place in oven. After about twenty minutes (fish should flake when prodded with fork), transfer fish and topping to heated platter, cover with foil and keep warm in turned-off oven. Strain and press ingredients from baking dish. Boil liquid remaining to reduce to about one-half cup. Beat egg yolk and cream together with wire whisk and when smooth whisk in one or two tablespoons of hot liquid, then pour egg and cream mixture into saucepan with remaining liquid, stirring constantly and simmer very gently (get it near a boil, and it will curdle) until the sauce thickens slightly. Stir in remaining tablespoon of butter and the lemon juice off the heat. Pour sauce over fish and serve.

BAKING

Almost any fish bakes well, but one of the top two or three has to be the summer-run steelhead trout. This particular fish provides topnotch baking characteristics and also lends itself to a variety of stuffings. The next time you wish to bake a large trout or summer steelhead, try cleaning the fish from the back instead of the belly. Simply cut from behind the head back along the backbone, cutting through the rib bones on one side of the backbone. Stop the cut even with the vent and remove the entrails and blood line. This method will provide the belly cavity as a pocket for stuffing the fish.

Here again let me urge you to experiment with varieties of ingredients for stuffing. The rule for salt when baking (pepper, too) is to *rub* the salt inside of the fish. If you don't, chances are the salt will be absorbed by the stuffing and not the fish.

Now, what to stuff the fish with? Well, almost any standard dressing used for fowl will do very well, as well different vegetables. Some have more affinity for fish than others. Lemon, onions, dill weed (dill pickles, too) all meld well with trout and salmon. Also, you might try rubbing the inside of the fish with hollandaise sauce or with a light coating of mayonnaise. I really go for a summer steelhead of five to seven pounds stuffed with layers of onions and sliced dill pickles with a tablespoon of pickle juices added for good measure.

Wrap the fish in foil, keeping the wrap somewhat loose, but sealing the foil as tightly as possible. Leave the head and tail on the fish. Bake in a hot oven (400°-425°) for about 45 minutes (five to seven pound fish), then slit the foil open and return to oven for another 10-15 minutes. Use a cookie sheet or shallow pan for the fish to collect any leakage. Open the foil and serve. Try using a metal spatula to serve. The meat will be tender, moist and flaky and will be easily removed from the bones.

Baked Fish in Herb Sauce (Salmon or Steelhead):

Sauce

8 ounce can Tomato Sauce	1 tsp. Lemon Juice
¼ cup Water or White Wine (sauterne or chablis)	½ tsp. Basil
	½ tsp. Thyme
2 tbsp. Oil or Melted Butter	

Bring sauce to a boil and simmer for five minutes. Pour well-mixed sauce over fish (fillets or steaks) in shallow baking pan and bake in 350° oven for thirty minutes. Sauce is sufficient for six servings of fish.

LOX

One very popular way of preparing salmon is with a "wet" smoke. The method is simple, the result delicious, and you end up with an item that would cost you $5 or $6 a pound to buy. To make lox you need some salmon cut into chunks (large); preferably the fish should be over fifteen pounds, and you should use only the thick center cuts. A plastic bucket or crock will do for storage. One box (7½ pounds) of Morton's Sugar Cure is needed (see your local Morton's Salt distributor).

Fillet your fish and remove the bone from three or four pieces taken from the thickest part of the fish. Put a generous handful of sugar cure in the bottom of the container and rub each piece of fish heavily with cure. Stack into layers skin-to-skin and meat-to-meat with a generous handful of cure between each layer. Sprinkle extra cure on top. Weight fish with a plate and a clean rock. Cover and remove to cool area (preferably one that does not get above 68° to 70°). Let stand for about eight weeks before use. However, the lox should be checked every two or three weeks for sugar mold. Sometimes a white mold will form (sugar mold). This mold is harmless but should be skimmed off with a slotted spoon. After eight weeks the liquid formed by the cure should cover the fish. If extra liquid is needed, mix three tablespoons of cure to one cup of water and pour over fish—continue until covered by liquid. Lox will store (under proper temperature conditions) almost indefinitely, but you must continue to check the liquid level—it must cover the fish!

When ready to use soak the fish out in cold water overnight, changing the water once. Lox can be sliced and served with crackers or served with rye bread or bagels and cream cheese, or it may be served hot by cutting into squares (one inch) and adding to new potatoes just before (five minutes or so) they are done. Also try adding lox to scrambled eggs. After soaking out, a piece of lox will keep for about two weeks in the refrigerator.

LOMI-LOMI SALMON

Jerry Erhammer, a reporter for the *Eugene Register Guard*, provided this delicious recipe:

Any of the salmonids will fit here. Fillet, skin and remove the rib bones from two or three pieces of fish. Cut into half-inch squares. Place fish in plastic bowl and add the squeezings of three limes (lemons may be used for a different flavor treat). Refrigerate overnight. Add the following:

1 Sweet Onion, finely chopped	generous amount Salt and Pepper
1-2 Tomatoes, finely chopped	3-5 drops of Tabasco

Refrigerate after mixing ingredients together for four to eight hours. Serve on crackers or as a topping for a green salad. Wow, it's good!

GENERAL COMMENTS

Included in this chapter is a recipe for brine for smoked salmon. One real taste treat for you to try is to use the brine as a pre-soak for barbequed salmon or steelhead. The next time you smoke, try pulling five or six pieces of fish out of the brine after ten or fifteen minutes and barbequing them.

When you cook fish over charcoal, the fish should be cooked skin-side down, fast, and not turned. If you have a tub type of cooker, you won't have any problems, but with a regular barbeque unit it will help to lay a large piece of aluminum foil over the fish (loosely) to help hold the heat. The skin will blacken and char, but the meat will cook evenly and be delicious.

The recipes included here are by no means even a small cross-section of the varieties of ways to prepare salmon and steelhead. However, all have been tested and have been found to be a combination of both different and delightful. Many people contributed to this particular section, but I am deeply indebted to three fishing buddies for a great deal of help. Jim Regan, Will Stensland and Bob Boryer all need to read this book thoroughly for more help with their fishing, although their cooking help was without peer!

Additionally, I thank the University of Alaska's Cooperative Extension Service for the use of their publication, *The Fisherman Returns*, and Harry Ragsdale of Oregon Mutual Savings Bank for loaning me one of the few copies in existence.